Gospel Values

for

Catholic Schools

a practical guide for today

CONTENTS

DEDICATION

*To the family
of Saint Gregory's Catholic College, Bath,
my school of formation*

BY THE SAME AUTHOR

Seeing the River (Edinburgh: Polygon, 1995)

Southfields, Vols 1–6, ed. with Richard Price (London: Southfields Press, 1995–2000)

Renfrewshire in Old Photographs, with Richard Price (Glasgow: Mariscat, 2000)

PS, Nos 1–7, ed. with Richard Price (London: Richard Price, 2006–2012)

Stations of the Heart (Cambridge: Salt, 2008)

How to Survive Working in a Catholic School, with Sister Judith Russi (Chawton: Redemptorist Publications, 2013)

How to Survive in Leadership in a Catholic School (Chawton: Redemptorist Publications, 2015)

The Revolution of Tenderness: Being a Catholic in Today's Church (Chawton: Redemptorist Publications, 2016)

The Hope that is Within You: Timothy Radcliffe in Conversation with Raymond Friel, CD and Transcript (Chawton: Redemptorist Publications, 2016)

FOREWORD

It is a privilege to be invited to write the foreword for a book which constitutes a timely publication in an era when Gospel values, which have always been at the heart of Catholic education, are being challenged in a rapidly changing context. Raymond Friel brings his vast experience of Catholic educational leadership to bear in addressing the centrality of Gospel values in the current climate in which the very existence of schools with a religious character, which pre-date state schools, is increasingly being challenged.

As the title suggests, Friel's account is rooted firmly in the Gospels and encompasses a coherent narrative of the significance of Gospel values for the Catholic school in general and its leadership in particular. The chapters entitled *Eight Signs of a Gospel-inspired School* and *Eight Signs of Gospel-inspired Leadership* are particularly pertinent in an era dominated by performativity, emphasising Christ "as the foundation of the whole education enterprise" and, by definition, focusing on the criticality of witness which is embedded within the tradition of Catholic education, particularly since the introduction of mass education in the nineteenth century. St John Bosco inspired hundreds of Salesians to embark upon the Catholic education project by means of his bright and joyful witness of what he proclaimed, a successful and

attractive Christian model capable of combining faith and life. Friel suggests that such models, committed to living rather than laminating Gospel values, are essential for the flourishing of the Catholic education project. The inclusion of reflections by leaders of Catholic education across the sector at the end of each chapter constitutes a particularly positive feature and ensures that the book combines effectively both theory and practice.

As the vice chancellor of a Catholic university in which the formation of Catholic teachers stands at its core, I enthusiastically recommend this book to the Catholic education community. Its content has a range of applications at both a strategic and an operational level and it is, therefore, essential reading for diocesan leaders, governors and Catholic school leaders alongside those charged with the formation of Catholic school leaders and teachers. I would also commend this book to the reading lists of qualifications such as the Catholic Certificate in Religious Studies and the St Mary's University MA in Catholic School Leadership.

Francis Campbell

INTRODUCTION

This book is in many ways a companion piece to *How to Survive in Leadership in a Catholic School*. In that book, my focus was on the role of the head teacher and on trying to provide practical advice and guidance for my colleagues on what the role involved and how to survive and thrive in the increasingly challenging environment of school and college leadership. I interviewed sixteen heads and principals, and their lived experience of the role provided much wisdom and insight.

In this book I have attempted to answer two questions which I believe will be of further assistance to Catholic leaders and aspiring leaders in education. First, why should Catholic schools and colleges continue to exist at all? There are increasingly confident voices in our society who claim that faith-based education is outdated and divisive. There are many people calling for a national conversation about the values we stand for as a society, with the starting point that none of those values can be based on the transcendent. In an age when so much violence is done in the name of God, it suits many people to consider God as part of the problem. We need to join that debate and give an account of what inspires our vision – the Gospel of Jesus Christ and the vision of God presented there which, as Pope Francis says, is a vision of a God of mercy and compassion.

Our values should be based on the Gospel, and that prompts my second question: what are Gospel values and how can they be applied in our schools? Like many Catholics, for me the Bible was not always the first place I turned to for spiritual direction. In Catholic education we talk about the importance of Gospel values, but not always with much detailed reference back to the Gospels. I have drawn on reliable Catholic biblical scholarship and advice from the Bishops' Conference to help me to establish a list of ten Gospel values and then suggested some questions to help Catholic leaders evaluate the extent to which these values are a reality in the life of the school.

We also need to make it clear that our education system, far from doing harm to young people and the wider society, is a force for good. We have impressive figures for the educational outcomes of our schools and colleges (see http://www.catholiceducation.org.uk for more information, including the digests of 2015 census data), but more than that, we have a very long tradition of contributing to the common good. As the Church documents and our own experience show, we have always been committed to the good of society and to producing good citizens. The Catholic Church is not some cult with secretive schools dedicated to producing "good Catholics" who will take their place in society as plotters against the State.

We can prove that our schools are effective in educational outcomes, and we can show that our attitude to the wider society has always been one of service and contribution. Where we are lacking is in showing the impact of our values-based education in the adult lives of our students. In common with other schools, we currently measure the impact of our education at the point when students leave us. What some of our academic commentators are now calling for is longitudinal research to show the effects of a Catholic education on the values and life choices of our former students. Do students who were educated in Catholic schools and colleges retain and develop a commitment to the common good in their adult lives? Schools and colleges could consider undertaking their own versions of that research through surveys with former students. This would be a considerable help to our cause.

In the meantime, we can strengthen our understanding of our mission and purpose by discerning even more deeply what a school inspired by the Gospel should be like and by articulating the ways in which we continue to offer a service to our community. To help me in this work, I interviewed thirteen leaders in Catholic education. I felt it was important not just to interview head teachers but to draw upon the experience and wisdom of our colleagues in higher education, in academic research and in our diocesan offices. I also felt it was important to hear the voices of leaders from the maintained and independent sectors as well as from non-maintained special schools. The Church has always insisted that different types of Catholic schools, under the direction of their local bishop, all have the same educational mission. Our special

schools, in particular, seem to me to be very close to Jesus' preferential option for the most vulnerable. We would do well to hear more about their exemplary work.

I have resisted the temptation to end each chapter with evaluative questions, with the exception of Chapter 3. Schools and colleges will have their own evaluative frameworks provided by their dioceses, based on the Section 48 inspection process. The eight signs of a Gospel-inspired school and Gospel-inspired leadership may provide some useful prompts to improve practice. Since there is not much detailed work on Gospel values I felt it was appropriate to provide some evaluative questions on each of the values, as well as exemplars of each, which I hope proves to be helpful. This is all just part of a conversation, an attempt to grow in wisdom, and the more of our colleagues who can be given opportunities to contribute to that conversation the better.

CHAPTER 1

Values or Virtues: where do we begin?

– CHAPTER 1 –

Values or Virtues: where do we begin?

As a serving head teacher, when I looked at my students at assembly on a Monday morning I saw hundreds of happy, well-rounded, quirky, funny, bright, talented young people. However, I also knew that among them there was a wide range of needs and some troubled backgrounds. The consensus among my peers in leadership is that those needs are growing at an exponential rate. More of our young people coming through the school system today seem to be unsettled, even angry, and directionless, venting their frustrations against an adult world that appears to have given up on them. *Toxic Childhood* by Sue Palmer, published in 2006, captured the sense of crisis. A "perfect storm" of online overstimulation, bad diet, poor exercise, disturbed sleep, weak parenting, exam stress and low self-esteem was pushing our young people towards self-destructive behaviour. Palmer put her finger on a deeper issue which has continued to preoccupy the adult world: "Moral guidance has suffered as societies become increasingly confused, while children are constantly exposed to manipulative advertising and the excesses of celebrity culture."[1]

An unexpected outbreak of urban rioting in English cities in 2011 brought the issues of disaffected youth into the national spotlight. The Prime Minister David Cameron gave a speech in response to the riots in which he identified a "slow motion moral collapse"[2] as the source of the disorder. He abandoned any pretence of moral neutrality from the government and declared that "this was about behaviour… people showing indifference to right and wrong… people with a twisted moral code… people with a complete absence of self-restraint."[3] It is a fascinating speech in many ways. The Prime Minister had to deal with his own discomfort in raising moral issues but clearly came to the conclusion that this was the only meaningful language in which to address what had happened. The secular State had to talk morals. What followed was a search for the moral framework a pluralistic society could sign up to. Some analysts and academics brought our attention back to the language of virtue, which has seen a significant revival in the academic community in the last fifty years or so. Recent government publications have picked up on this, with an emphasis on character education.

Before we consider the essential elements of good character or virtue, and whether or not that is the best approach for Catholic schools, let's consider what good mental health and well-being looks like since this might take us closer to the root of the problem. Young Minds (http://youngminds.org.uk) is a leading UK charity committed to improving the emotional well-being and mental health of children and young people. The charity campaigns, researches and seeks to influence policy and practice at both local and national level. Its annual report for 2014/15 begins with a definition of emotional resilience and good mental health that includes the following:

• The capacity to enter into and sustain mutually satisfying personal relationships

• A continuing progression of psychological development

• An ability to play and to learn appropriately for their age and intellectual level

• A developing moral sense of right and wrong

• The capacity to cope with a degree of psychological distress

• A clear sense of identity and self-worth

• The ability to "bounce back" in the face of adversity.[4]

Everyone I know in leadership in education would sign up to that list and would regard the points as "standard" in the life of their schools. Many of the Prime Minister's concerns would be addressed if those bullet points described a daily reality for our young people. Catholic education, which has been my educational *habitus*, would embrace those definitions of good mental health and, moreover, bring a rich

resource of Church teaching to any discussion of how they might be understood and implemented. The problem we are facing in education and society in general is that too many young people fall well short of those definitions of good mental health. This generally does not lead to rioting, but it does manifest itself in many harmful ways which can include anti-social behaviour on a smaller scale. Young Minds claims in its annual report that:

• 850,000 children and young people in the UK have a clinically significant mental health problem

• 1 in 10 children aged 5–16 years, or 3 in every classroom, experience mental health problems, a figure which has doubled between the 1980s and the 2000s

• 60% of Looked After Children have emotional or mental health problems and are six times more likely to have a conduct disorder and four times more likely to attempt suicide

• 1 in 12 young people self-harm, and since 2002 there has been a 68% increase in the number of hospital admissions of young people self-harming

• 95% of imprisoned young offenders have a mental health disorder.[5]

So what is causing so many young people to self-harm, to find themselves labelled with a "conduct disorder" or to consider taking their own lives? And where do we begin to look for a solution? Let us stay for the time being with those secular agencies which are on the front line and have no vested interest in political ideology. What do they think are the factors which have led to such a worrying decline in the behaviour and well-being of our young people? Young Minds says that it is because:

• family breakdown is widespread

• there is so much pressure to have access to money, the perfect body and lifestyle

• materialist culture heavily influences young people

• 24-hour social networking and what young people can access from a young age can have a negative impact on their mental health and well-being

• body image is a source of much distress for many young people

• bullying both on- and offline is rife

• increasing sexual pressures and early sexualisation throw young people into an adult world they don't understand

• violence is rife in many communities and fear of crime a constant source of distress for thousands of young people

• schools are getting more and more like exam factories; university entry has become more competitive and expensive

• 13% of 16–24-year-olds are not in employment, education or training (NEET).[6]

None of the above will come as much of a surprise. There are some aspects of those challenges which we in education can do little about, such as the pervasive force of the materialistic and hedonistic culture of the West. We can, however, and in many cases do, run our schools as "health centres of the spirit" to offer prevention if not cure for the lures of materialism and "false" body images and the effects of online bullying and sexualised behaviour, and give our students every opportunity to discover their "vocation" and what they might do with their one precious life. There are other points in that list which should give us serious pause for thought: are our schools "exam factories" which cause stress in our students? It is a pernicious dilemma, as school leaders find themselves under increasing pressure to perform or perish – but at what cost? As we will see later, the Church has always promoted a "rounded education" and considers academic success as important, but only as part of a Catholic approach to education.

Compromised Authority

Before we go any further in deciding on the solutions to the problems facing our young people, it is worth pointing out that the old narrative of responsible adults deciding what is best for troubled youth is now deeply flawed, as acknowledged by the Prime Minister in that speech about the riots. Adults are in fact part of the problem. Adult institutions in recent years have been exposed one after another as having deep-seated problems of child abuse, corruption and incompetence. The Independent Inquiry into Child Sexual Abuse (https://www.iicsa.org.uk/) has proposed twelve investigations to cover a range of institutions, including local authorities, specific residential homes and the Anglican and Catholic Churches, as well as looking into abuse by persons of public prominence. It is a source of deep shame that respected institutions, including the Catholic Church, have not done nearly enough to protect young people in their care from sexual abuse by their members. That is why safeguarding in all our Catholic institutions must be not only compliant, but exemplary.

As well as the scandals of abuse, some adults have caused economic mayhem by their greed and dishonesty. In 2008, the financial system was brought close to collapse by the actions of a few (and if we are honest, by the willing participation of many more who were happy to live on absurd amounts of credit). The film *The Big Short* (2015), based on the book *The Big Short: inside the Doomsday Machine* (2010) by Michael Lewis, is a brilliant and profoundly disturbing account of how the crisis was triggered by the housing bubble in the USA. We have been paying for it ever since, with austerity programmes across the western world bringing further misery, often to the most vulnerable. Some adults who worked in journalism were found to be deliberately tapping the phones of members of the public in order to generate news stories. Some adults who were democratically elected to serve in Parliament were found to be cheating the system by making personal gain out of expenses claims. One after another, cracks have appeared in the façades of the institutions which for centuries have defined public standards and influenced public opinion. It is little wonder that some commentators refer to the "end of deference".

As we pronounce on what values or virtues are best

for our young people with their current problems, therefore, we should look first at ourselves, the adults who run the system, and adopt a posture of some humility. Rule by the unaccountable patriarchs who knew best has been found wanting. In recent years the Catholic Church, for one, has adopted a stance of much greater humility. Vatican II set the tone with a new outreach to the people of the modern world, a new warmth and sense of service. Pope Saint John XXIII, in his address to the opening session of the Council in October 1962, said: "The great desire, therefore, of the Catholic Church in raising aloft at this Council the torch of truth, is to show herself to the world as the loving mother of all mankind; gentle, patient, and full of tenderness and sympathy for her separated children."[7]

Church Councils in the past were often convened to combat a particular heresy and concluded by issuing a condemnation (*anathema*) of the heresy in question. Vatican II was unique in that it was not convened to counteract a heresy. John XXIII, in that memorable opening address, wanted the world to know that the purpose and tone of this gathering was quite different: "The Church has always opposed errors, and often condemned them with the utmost severity. Today, however, Christ's bride prefers the balm of mercy to the arm of severity."[8]

Pope Francis has reinforced this message, in particular with the Year of Mercy in 2015/16. He takes us back repeatedly to the source of our faith, Jesus Christ, and to his words and deeds as passed down to us by the Gospels. To the wider world the Church has often seemed to be absorbed in a labyrinth of regulations and rituals. Pope Francis brings Jesus, the merciful face of the Father, back to the centre of our attention: "The signs he works, especially in favour of sinners, the poor, the marginalized, the sick, and the suffering, are all meant to teach mercy. Everything in him speaks of mercy. Nothing in him is devoid of compassion."[9] There can be no doubt for those working in Catholic education about what our response should be to the problems of the age, who our priority should be, where we should look for inspiration and what attitude we should adopt in our work.

In Mark's Gospel, there is a moving story which shows the extent of the compassion of Jesus for the crowds. He has just heard that his great friend and mentor John the Baptist has been executed by Herod. He is exhausted trying to keep up with the pace of his own ministry. He needs a break and invites his disciples to "come away to a deserted place all by yourselves and rest a while" (Mark 6:31). They go off in a boat to find a quiet spot for some "downtime", as we might say today. The crowd has other ideas, and a mass of people is there waiting for them. Instead of sending them away, which would be quite understandable, Mark tells us that Jesus "had compassion for them, because they were like sheep without a shepherd; and he began to teach them many things" (Mark 6:34). This passage could be an exemplum for Catholic leaders in education. So many of our young people are like sheep without a shepherd, longing for meaning and healing. So many of us leaders are exhausted and feel the need to get away. Jesus does not turn his back on the needy crowd. He has compassion, he teaches, he heals, and he keeps doing that until the end. It is a loving self-emptying, or *kenosis*.

Empty Jars

We have looked briefly at the nature of the problems facing our young people and reminded ourselves of the "well" we should always return to as Catholic educators when looking for nourishment and inspiration. The Church over the years has often contributed to the analysis of the problems facing modern society, but alas with severity and condemnation. In recent times, however, the commentary has been less of a jeremiad, and more in line with the compassionate stance urged by John XXIII and Francis. *New Vocations for a New Europe*, published by the Pontifical Work for Ecclesiastical Vocations in 1997, addresses directly the concerns of young people and describes a situation not dissimilar to the challenges outlined above. The document places great emphasis on *accompanying* the young people in our care and refers to the haunting story of the two disheartened disciples on the road to Emmaus after the death of Jesus: "it seems to us that, in the two disciples, it is possible to see the image of many young people today, a little saddened and betrayed, who have lost the desire to look for their vocation".[10]

The young people are indeed a little sad and feel betrayed by many of the adults in their lives. The document is humble enough to acknowledge that young people do not always see in the Church the answer to their questions: for them "God is not the problem, the Church is."[11] The irony is that the Church describes the plight of young people in a language resonant of the rich resources that many are turning their back on. The authors refer to another story of transformative encounter in the Gospels, between a tired and thirsty Jesus and a socially isolated Samaritan woman at Jacob's well (John 4:1–42), to elaborate on the theme of accompaniment:

> To accompany a young person means knowing how to identify the "wells" of today; all of those places and moments, those provocations and expectations where, sooner or later, all young people must pass with their empty jars, with their unspoken questions, with their obstinate, often only apparent self-sufficiency, with their deep-seated desire for authenticity and the future.[12]

It is a beautifully sad image: our young people with their "empty jars" looking for meaning, answers, looking for someone or something to believe in when all they are offered is the transience of materialism and celebrity. So what can we offer them, what do we have to fill their jars? Hopefully a set of values or virtues so attractive that they will cling on to them for the rest of their lives.

This takes us close to the root of the problem we started with: how can we as representatives of a compromised adult world identify any set of values or virtues which young people can believe in? The very notion of moral authority is met with suspicion. The two great fallacies of the modern age identified by *New Vocations* – the claim of subjectivity and the desire for freedom – work against any set of values or virtues claiming an absolute foundation or reference point. Modern Europe is likened to the pantheon of ancient Rome in which "all the 'divinities' are present, or in which every 'value' has its place and its niche".[13] This feature of modern society was memorably

described by Pope Benedict XVI as the "tyranny of relativism", or, as in the title of the Manic Street Preachers' album, *This Is My Truth Tell Me Yours*. The authors of *New Vocations* elaborate on the impact of this feature of modern life:

> When a culture no longer defines the supreme possibilities of meaning, or does not manage to converge around certain values as particularly capable of giving meaning to life, but places everything on the same level… everything becomes indifferent and flat.[14]

Good Character

So what values can we offer our young people to give them some hope of meaning in life, to give them some sense of identity and self-worth, to help them to "flourish" and to grow into the human beings God wants them to be? What "counter-narrative" can we provide against the dominant script that says that possessions, prestige and power are what life is all about? And are we offering values or virtues? The Church has talked about both, although there is a longer tradition of talking about virtues. But before we look at what the Church has to say about virtues and values, let us go back to the secular domain and see how the agenda has developed in recent years.

The State stepped into the narrative of values with dramatic effect in June 2011 when the then Home Secretary, Theresa May MP, launched the Prevent Strategy. This was in response not to the riots, which had not yet erupted on our streets, but to the growing threat of terrorist attacks, the radicalisation of young British citizens in terrorist causes and the role of a small number of schools in that radicalisation. In the education section of the Strategy it was noted that "there have been allegations that a minority of independent faith schools have been actively promoting views that are contrary to British values, such as intolerance of other cultures and gender inequality".[15] Schools were identified as one of the fronts in the ideological battle against the extremists. The gauge that was used to distinguish schools which were showing bias towards the extremists was the extent to which they supported or undermined British values.

In November 2014 the Department for Education (DfE) published guidance for maintained schools which confirmed the requirement that "schools should promote the fundamental British values of democracy, the rule of law, individual liberty, and mutual respect of those with different faiths and beliefs".[16] In the same year the DfE launched a short consultation to revise the Independent School Standards to include the provision that free schools, academies and independent schools should also *actively promote* fundamental British values. We will look in more detail at British values in Chapter 6, and in particular at how Catholic schools might respond to this new requirement in the light of their own value system.

Following on from the focus on values, the government in the years following the riots of 2011 also began to use the language of character and character education. The most recent articulation of the government's vision for the education of the nation's young people was published in March 2016

as a White Paper (a policy document produced by the government that sets out its proposals for future legislation, as opposed to a Green Paper, which is a consultation document produced by the government to receive feedback on proposals for legislation) entitled *Educational Excellence Everywhere*. The White Paper states:

> A 21st century education should prepare children for adult life by instilling the character traits and fundamental British values that will help them succeed: being resilient and knowing how to persevere, how to bounce back if faced with failure, and how to collaborate with others at work and in their private lives…These traits not only open doors to employment and social opportunities but underpin academic success, happiness and well-being.[17]

A straight line can be drawn from the Prime Minister's decision in 2011 to adopt a discourse of morality and the White Paper's confidence to define the values and character traits which lead to happiness and well-being. I have been a head teacher in maintained schools for fourteen years and I have generally supported the government's priorities in education, but I'm bound to say that the government's most recent vision for its young people leaves me distinctly underwhelmed. Its list of character traits which, along with British values, will help young people to succeed in life seems to me very limited. Of course, resilience, perseverance and collaboration are important (and featured in that list of mental health attributes from Young Minds), but it seems such a cautious and incomplete list. Are these traits really enough to bring happiness and well-being? There is much more to be said about the human person than "Keep calm and carry on".

As for British values, as a serving head teacher I have actively promoted them and worked to understand them in the light of the mission of my Catholic school, but I'm not inspired by them, my life has not been turned around by them, I wouldn't go the wall for them. And what is the vision of a human life held out to our young people by this document? It seems to be limited to "employment and social opportunities", which, again, are good things to be wished for, but in the thinking of the Catholic Church on education, there is more to life than that. There is much in the White Paper to be commended, including a strong emphasis on equality and social justice, but as a vision of human flourishing it is not a rich or compelling document.

Other groups and organisations have developed a deeper understanding of character education and virtues. One of the most prominent is the Jubilee Centre for Character and Virtue, based at the University of Birmingham. In 2015 the Centre published a major research report into character and virtue education in schools, involving more than 10,000 students in 68 schools across the UK. The Centre has a much broader understanding of character education than that espoused by the White Paper. It considers good character to include moral virtues (honesty and kindness), civic virtues (community service), intellectual virtues (curiosity and creativity) and performance virtues (diligence and perseverance). It registers concerns that "in some academic and political circles, 'character' has recently come to be equated only with the possession of performance virtues such as resilience and self-confidence".[18] This was written before the White Paper was published, of course, so it is not a direct reference to that.

The report proposes that the renewed interest in character education (whose origins date back to Aristotle's *Ethics*) arises from "a widespread sense that the moral fabric of society is unravelling".[19] It quotes the work of the sociologist Christian Smith, author of the influential book *Lost in Translation: the dark side of emerging adulthood*. Smith's research, based in America, led him to conclude that "we are failing to teach and model moral reasoning skills, visions of a good life that transcends material consumption and immediate bodily pleasures, and the importance of participation in public life for the common good."[20] This is an intriguing point for Catholic educators, for whom such a vision should be integral to their mission. The work of the Jubilee Centre is a serious and worthy attempt to promote character education in its richest meaning. Its vision is the creation of a good society through the practice of virtue. It is involved in a number of innovative projects across not just schools but various professions aimed at promoting virtuous behaviour.

My main question about character education in its best manifestation is this: what are the foundations and criteria for arriving at the virtues? In a section on the background to character education, the report quoted above acknowledges that a "variety of moral theories have been propounded and discussed since the eighteenth century"[21] before European philosophers returned to Aristotle's ethical ideas in the second half of the twentieth century. But what makes Aristotle's "virtue ethics" more secure than any other enlightened approach? The report goes on to say that "among the central tenets of an Aristotelian approach [is] the principle that there is an objective notion of human flourishing."[22] I cannot find in Aristotle, or in any other philosopher, an objective notion of human flourishing. As a Christian, the only place I can conceivably find an objective grounding for the human good is in the Gospel of Jesus Christ. So while the work on character education, especially as promoted by the Jubilee Centre, is important and will certainly contribute to the common good, for Catholic educators it can only provide an incomplete vision.

The Greatest of These is Love

To discover the thinking of the Catholic Church on the subject of virtues, a good place to start is the Catechism. I would say in passing that the Catechism of the Catholic Church has been left behind by many adults who associate it with the rote learning of their childhood. To come back to the Catechism in later life is, in my experience, to discover the proverbial treasure buried in the field. On the subject of virtues, the Catechism distinguishes between human, or moral, virtues and theological virtues. A virtue is defined as "an habitual and firm disposition to do the good. It allows the person not only to perform good acts, but to give of himself."[23] Human virtues are "firm attitudes, stable dispositions, habitual perfections of intellect that will govern our actions".[24] There are four human virtues that play a pivotal role and hence are known as the "cardinal"

virtues. They are prudence, justice, fortitude and temperance. For a definition of each, refer to paragraphs 1806–1811 of the Catechism.

The human virtues are acquired by education and by doing them. This has been the emphasis of the Church's educational establishments for centuries and there is no reason why modern Catholic establishments should take a different view. We need to continue to educate our young people in the language and examples of human virtues, but we have a very different perspective on the human person. We do not "achieve" virtue, or a virtuous existence, by our own efforts. What the Church brings to this debate is an acute sense of the fragility of the human condition, or, as we used to say, original sin. Still using the old exclusive language, the Catechism says that "it is not easy for man, wounded by sin, to maintain moral balance".[25] We need the "grace of light and strength"[26] and the life of the Church to help us on the right path. The secular model of virtue is bereft of any theological understanding of the fragility of people or the strength available from divine assistance. In the Catholic tradition we acknowledge our weakness (mea culpa) and dependence on God.

The human virtues, then, are rooted in what are known as theological virtues and these in essence adapt our faculties for "participation in the divine nature"[27] which is our ultimate end. The theological virtues are faith, hope and charity, or love. These form the foundation of Christian moral activity; they are the engine room, if you like, of the virtuous life. These virtues make us capable of acting like God's children, and again they are not acquired by our own efforts. They are gifts of God, and as St Paul said in his beautiful hymn to the theological virtues, "the greatest of these is love" (1 Corinthians 13:1–13). The Catechism tells us that all the virtues are "animated and inspired by charity".[28] This I think brings us to the heart of the matter. Jesus became flesh to tell us that the very nature of God is love, an insight captured by John's first letter (1 John 4:8). Jesus not only revealed the nature of God but told us that this is how we should live from now on, in what we call the *mandatum novum*, the new commandment: "Just as I have loved you, you also should love one another" (John 13:34).

This is what we should be putting in front of our young people in our Catholic schools – the "Christian version of reality".[29] To live a life of love, in love with God and our neighbour, is what we believe constitutes emotional and spiritual health in a human being. As Pope Francis said in *Evangelii Gaudium*, ("The Joy of the Gospel"), "life grows by being given away, and it weakens in isolation and comfort."[30] It is a profoundly *counter-cultural* message, although it is not *anti-social*. It provides our young people with a vision of life based on service, especially for the poor and vulnerable, modelled by Jesus throughout his ministry and at the last supper in John's Gospel: "so if I, your Lord and Teacher, have washed your feet, you also ought to wash one another's feet" (John 13:14). This should help us to consider virtues in their proper perspective, as the kind of behaviour which arises out of a loving life. The question for Catholic educators remains: what is the best way to unfold this truth to our young people in the course of their years with us? What should be our language and our framework?

If the universal Church will always guide us with a rich source of teaching, then the local Church will also provide guidance according to our own circumstances. In England and Wales, the most recent guidance on these issues supported by the Bishops' Conference of England and Wales is the publication *Christ at the Centre* by Monsignor (now Bishop) Marcus Stock. In this publication, Bishop Stock provides us with a helpful summary of the distinctive features of a Catholic school. He uses the term "Gospel values" a number of times and counters the argument that values are a modern subjective parlance which should be dropped in favour of the more reliable language of virtue. In fact, Bishop Stock uses both when he says that Catholic schools should "foster conduct and behaviour governed, ordered and guided by the four cardinal virtues and rooted in Gospel values".[31] The Catholic school, therefore, should not only promote Gospel values as part of the core of its purpose and mission but "integrate Gospel values and the teaching of the Catholic Church into every aspect of learning, teaching and the totality of school life".[32]

In a brief discussion of the history of values, Bishop Stock acknowledges that in common usage, values are often considered to be subjective, as in one's personal values. He reminds us that the German philosopher Nietzsche (1844–1900) used the term "values" in opposition to objective moral law. For him, "there were no objective virtues or vices, good or evil, right or wrong that are true for all time".[33] Values for him were subjective and referred to whatever an individual considered to be right or wrong, true or false, at any point in time. The term "Gospel values", then, is in danger of being treated the same way if we are not careful. We need an objective Christian foundation for these values, and for that Bishop Stock turns to the Beatitudes since they "depict the countenance of Jesus Christ and portray his charity".[34] In other words, the Beatitudes take us to the heart of the message of Christ and his "values" – what he stood for, what he believed to be the nature of reality, what he was "into", as the kids might say.

So with the confidence of that encouragement, we will continue to explore Gospel values, while acknowledging the central importance of the cardinal and theological virtues. *The Catholic School*, published by the Congregation for Catholic Education in 1977 as a fuller exposition of the Church's position on education following on from the general principles outlined in Vatican II's *Declaration on Christian Education*, goes so far as to say that "the Catholic school loses its purpose without constant reference to the Gospel and a frequent encounter with Christ".[35] We cannot focus on virtues at the expense of Gospel values, and those values find their objective expression in the life, death and resurrection of Jesus Christ, in what he said and did while he was with us and in what his encounters with human beings tell us about the nature of God.

A focus on Gospel values is also helpful from a "tactical" point of view since it allows us to join the national discussion about values prompted by the introduction of British values. It allows us all the more effectively to make our defence to anyone who demands from us "an accounting for the hope" (1 Peter 3:15) that is in us. And in recent times many have demanded to know what we stand for and some

have gone as far as to say that schools which are "rooted in the Gospel" should not exist in a secular society. *Living with Difference*, the report of the Commission on Religion and Belief in British Public Life published by the Cambridge-based Woolf Institute in 2015, called for "a national conversation to be launched across the UK by leaders of faith communities and ethical traditions to create a shared understanding of the fundamental values underlying public life".[36] This book is in part a response to that invitation, but for the most part it is an invitation to my colleagues in leadership in Catholic education to reflect with ever more depth and discernment on our mission, beginning as always with the Gospel of Jesus Christ.

Reflections by Leaders in Catholic Education

Among the leaders in Catholic education I interviewed, there was no clear consensus about whether it was the language of virtue or the language of values that should be adopted. However, it did seem as if the serving head teachers preferred the language of values, which they often regarded as institutional rather than personal, as a helpful framework for the overarching narrative of what they stood for and what informed their practice. The language of values was also seen as being closer to the discourse of today's society rather than the more traditional discourse of virtues. The language of virtues seemed to some to be more intellectually compelling but there was no corresponding framework from Church leaders for how Christian virtues might be used in practice, apart from the example of the

Jesuit schools. The most recent guidance from the Bishops' Conference of England and Wales, *Christ at the Centre*, strongly favoured the language of Gospel values, based on the Beatitudes of Matthew's Gospel, and provided a list of those values. In most of the mission statements of Catholic schools and colleges I have studied, the language of values is preferred to that of virtues, although there is no consistency in what constitutes these values.

◌

I've always thought that we don't really make enough use of the great repository of our saints. We have an absolute treasure-house of virtue in the saints and if they are used in the education of young people then virtues are made manifest in the person and that's very powerful. My great personal hero is St Thomas More. The virtue of integrity is what he had and he had a great deal to lose by standing up to somebody like King Henry VIII and he tried by every means not to be a martyr but in the end [uttered] that famous phrase of his which ought to be the phrase that governs all Catholic institutions, "We seek to be the King's good servant, but God's first", and I think we are not drawing on a great resource that we have, to talk about the virtues of the saints as exemplified in different situations.

You've got to always think when you're talking values, what is at the root of the value, where has it come from, why should anyone give it value status, why should they value it? In the case of Christianity, the values have their final authenticity in the word of God and in the life and teachings of Jesus Christ. That is their final

validation of significance and importance. A secular State can't do that. You can go so far as to say that Christ, in this country, is the foundation of these values. It's not the British State.

—Gerald Grace, Director of the Centre for Research and Development in Catholic Education, St Mary's, Twickenham

The advantage in doing this within a church setting is there can be an agreement or you can be clear on what Gospel values actually are: respect, love, charity, the whole range of clearly defined Gospel values. You can agree on what the Gospel values actually are or what decision has been taken. The next step is what that means in the context you find yourself in. How are you guided in the articulation? How do you create a respectful culture? How do you create a loving culture and how do you run an effective operation with all the other matrices that sit alongside that? How are Gospel values applied in a Catholic educational setting, how are values applied, how do we apply the professional norms and matrices that are demanded of us by the regulatory authorities and then ask ourselves, is there an imbalance here? Do we pay as much attention to the Catholic educational values, the Gospel values in the Catholic educational setting, as we would to, say, the requirements coming out from Ofsted? My guess would be there is an imbalance and it's not in favour of Gospel values.

—Francis Campbell, Vice-Chancellor of St Mary's University, Twickenham

In our schools in the province we did a piece of work around saying if you want to describe, in terms of virtue, the sort of young people that you want to form in our schools which are Catholic Christian in the Jesuit tradition, what virtues would you use? We came up with eight pairs of virtues, sixteen words altogether, and those come very, very clearly from the Gospel – faith, hope, love, compassion. Also we use the words "intentional" and "prophetic". They're not in the Gospel as such but they're concepts that come out of the Gospel, and then we would also choose words from the Ignatian tradition which hopefully is representing the Gospel, so it's not something different and distinct from it but it is a particular spiritual thread in western Christianity. So, for example, we would have "attentive" and "discerning", which is the basis of Ignatian spirituality, being attentive to your experience and then discerning a way forward from that. We also have, for example, "gratitude" and "generosity", which are the bookends of the spiritual exercises. Ignatius always begins with gratitude and what have I to be grateful for, and finishes with how do I use these gifts, and the answer is generously in the service of others. We picked out, as I say, sixteen words, eight pairs of words, which we refer to as virtues and that's the way in which we would articulate it. Tolerance is a virtue, it's a good virtue for government to promote, but it doesn't really have a place in Christianity because it's trumped by compassion and love, something that's far stronger and far deeper.

—Adrian Porter, Delegate for Education for the British Province of the Society of Jesus

"Gospel values" is a phrase that is used often but only makes sense within the matrix from which it emerges. So, trying to make sense of the word "values", apart from the network to which it belongs, is difficult. I would say that virtue is a stronger term. Virtues dwell in us whereas values, possibly, are more peripheral, like ethos and culture versus climate, climate being the more peripheral term. Virtues involve training, apprenticeship, community, communication, self-subordination, disposition, happiness, building on Thomas Aquinas in terms of his assimilation of Aristotle and virtue. So that is our starting point if we're going to talk about disposition in a Christian context.

—John Lydon, Programme Director for Catholic School Leadership, at St Mary's University, Twickenham

I think the other thing I would say about values as opposed to virtues, is that values are aspirational in some way. My value is that I wish to be forgiving but I don't always live up to that. I would say the virtue is when the value has become so ingrained that it shapes the pattern of my life and my days so that I don't have to call it in to mind, I just do it, I just live it. When I'm talking to young teachers and I'm talking about the difference between values and virtues one of the images I use is from *Finding Nemo*. There's a scene when the sharks have formed a self-help group and their value is that they no longer want to eat fish, they don't want to be cannibalistic and eat other fish. That's the value that they aspire to but at the slightest hint of blood, one of the sharks goes crazy and tries to consume the fish and eat them all. Therefore, he has the value but it hasn't become ingrained, it isn't a virtue, it isn't a habit of being. For me that's part of the difference. I think we name values that we hold to be true but it's living them out that becomes the virtuous life, the good life and where you take those values from makes a difference.

—Diocesan Officer, Catholic Diocesan Education Department

We recognise that we are a Catholic school because of the values that underpin what we do. We serve these children because they are unique. Amongst a range of young people, they are unique. Why do we do this? A special school down the road would do exactly the same, they work just as hard. It's the why that makes it different here. And I think, also, it's that willingness to operate out of love, and unashamedly so and name it as such and I feel that very much amongst the staff. You get that sense of them trying to love the learners, but also each other, because I think they recognise they're in an extreme situation. But I think it is a transforming and life-giving community, which is what you want a Catholic community to be.

—Dave Purcell, Head of Religious Studies, St Joseph's Special School, Cranleigh

The term "Gospel values" I believe is about how we create the kingdom of God here on earth; appreciating each person as unique, special and loved; celebrating the boundless

opportunities God has planned for them. Each individual, young and old, has a purpose regardless of their behaviour, attitude or ability and we as educators have to ensure they make their personal mark on the world. Every person is a light that needs to be allowed to shine and never be hidden away. At times it can be hard to find the light but our mission must be all about prayer, perseverance and hope.

—Clare Hogg, Headteacher, St Thomas More Catholic High School, Crewe

This whole question about character education is very interesting, although in all the literature I've read from the Jubilee Centre, which is quite rigorous in its empirical basis for what it tries to say, they don't seem to touch very much on theological virtues. They concentrate very much on something which is perhaps common to every culture. You could argue that Aristotle's cardinal virtues would make for a better society in any culture, pagan, Christian, eastern, western. Justice, good sense, moderation and courage would be valued, potentially, by any society, so I can see why they're focusing more on virtues which are common across cultures and across societies and they seem to have a lot of influence, talking to governments all over the world. It's very interesting but it doesn't really touch hugely on the virtues which would shape a Church and a Church school, which are more about faith, hope and love.

—Hugh Walters, Head of Theology, Downside School, Stratton-on-the-Fosse

I haven't ever used the word "virtues", actually, in any assemblies or RE lessons so I think it would be naming them in the way that we just have, to be a gentle person, to be a kind person, compassionate. We talk about them in that way with the pupils and then illustrate them with stories. I think that Gospel values are the values that make you a good follower of Jesus, the values that Jesus himself promoted and that we should be living out if we are true followers of Christ. When I'm summarising it to girls or to staff I usually say that "love, trust and respect" are the Gospel values that I think we should be showing.

—Sarah Conrad, Head of Prep School, St Teresa's, Effingham

Reflections from Scripture

Finally, beloved, whatever is true, whatever is honourable, whatever is just, whatever is pure, whatever is pleasing, whatever is commendable, if there is any excellence and if there is anything worthy of praise, think about these things. Keep on doing the things that you have learned and received and heard and seen in me, and the God of peace will be with you. (Philippians 4:8–9)

So they watched him and sent spies who pretended to be honest, in order to trap him by what he said, so as to hand him over to the jurisdiction and authority of the governor. So they asked him, "Teacher, we know that you are right in what you say and teach, and you show deference to no one, but teach the way of God in accordance with the truth. Is it lawful for us to pay taxes to the emperor, or not?" But he perceived their craftiness and said to them, "Show me a denarius. Whose head and whose title does it bear?" They said, "The emperor's." He said to them, "Then give to the emperor the things that are the emperor's, and to God the things that are God's." And they were not able in the presence of the people to trap him by what he said; and being amazed by his answer, they became silent. (Luke 20:20–26)

CHAPTER 2

Jesus: the parable of God

– CHAPTER 2 –

Jesus: the parable of God

If we are to say anything about Gospel values then we have to go back to the Gospels, not rely on second-hand interpretations. For hundreds of years up until the Second Vatican Council, the Gospel was proclaimed in Latin, so the Good News was heard but seldom understood. The focus was more on the teachings derived from the Gospel, the norms and precepts of the Church, with an emphasis on meritorious action leading to personal salvation. The Council's Dogmatic Constitution on Divine Revelation, *Dei Verbum*, promulgated in 1965, changed that culture when it declared that "easy access to Sacred Scripture should be provided for all the Christian faithful".[1] Translations and biblical scholarship were encouraged. For lay people, the intention was not just that they should have access to scripture – the Council fathers urged the Christian faithful "to learn by frequent readings of the divine Scriptures the 'excellent knowledge of Jesus Christ' (Phil. 3:8)",[2] for ignorance of the scriptures, as Saint Jerome said, is ignorance of Christ.

For Catholic leaders in education who are seeking a deeper insight into their mission, scripture is the place to begin, specifically the Gospels. It has taken me fourteen years as a Catholic head teacher to arrive at this insight. In the past, when I led school communities through a mission review process I generally started with the Church documents on Catholic education. These are important and will inform the community about the principles of Catholic education, but they are not the *source*. The point I overlooked for all those years is that we need to start with the Gospels. I suspect the reason I overlooked them is because the Church documents were easier to deal with: clear definitions of the Catholic school, neat lists of characteristics, user-friendly quotations to be extracted for my PowerPoint presentations. But it is all at one remove from the radical challenge of the Gospel.

The most recent document from the Congregation of Catholic Education, *Educating Today and Tomorrow: a renewing passion*, arrives at the same conclusion. It reflects on the end of deference we mentioned in the previous chapter and concludes that in this more challenging environment the authority of heads can no longer be based on formal rules but instead must be based on the power of their own testimony and witness: "Catholic schools must be run by individuals and teams who are inspired by the Gospel, who have been formed in Christian pedagogy, in tune with Catholic schools' educational project, and not by people who are prone to being seduced by fashionability."[3] That means we must read the Gospels before we read the documents on education. Not only read them, but allow them to touch us, inspire us, change us. Then we can lead a Gospel-inspired school.

We do not encounter ideas about God in the Gospels; rather, we encounter God Himself, as revealed in Jesus, who tells us of "the innermost being of God".[4] This is a knowledge which our society is losing, and part of our role as Catholic leaders is the urgent commission "to keep the memory of God made flesh in the history of mankind alive".[5] We will lose that memory ourselves unless we grow in understanding, through contemplation and study, of the words handed down from the apostolic tradition. As the Council fathers said, we receive the bread of life "from the table both of God's word and of Christ's body".[6] This is the same sustenance offered to those two despondent disciples on the road to Emmaus, following the death of Jesus (Luke 24:13–35). In that story, it's as if Luke wanted to reassure his own community, fifty years after the death of Jesus, that they had the same "daily bread" as the two disciples – the word of God as spoken by Jesus on the road and the body of Christ broken for them at the Eucharist.

Jesus in Luke's Gospel

When we turn our attention to the Gospels we find four very different texts. There is a consensus that Mark's account is the oldest Gospel (c. AD 70). It may have been written for a community in travail, perhaps the Christian community in Rome under

Nero's persecution. Everybody in the Gospel seems to fail, apart from Jesus. In the original ending the women flee from the empty tomb, "for they were afraid…" (Mark 16:8). Matthew and Luke's Gospel (c. AD 85) both use Mark's Gospel as a source but produce different accounts, because they are writing for very different communities. Matthew is conscious of his Jewish audience and conscious too of the wealthy members of his community, who were no doubt a helpful resource. The rich in Matthew, like Joseph of Arimathaea (Matthew 27:57) are presented as disciples like everybody else. Luke seems to struggle with the rich, or at least he sees wealth as a serious obstacle to discipleship. John's Gospel (c. AD 95) bears the scars of polemical battles with the synagogue and from the beginning takes for granted what the other Gospels struggled towards: Jesus is the pre-existent Word of God.

Rather than trying to range across all four Gospels, then, it seems more useful to get to know Jesus as presented in one Gospel since they are all different in terms of emphasis. For many years Matthew was favoured as the "teaching Gospel" of the Church, since so much of its content reflected the beliefs and experience of an early Church community. For our purposes, however, I would like to concentrate on Luke's Gospel, in part because it seems so much in tune with the kind of Church Pope Francis is urging us to become again: a Church of mercy, a Church for the poor. Luke more than any other evangelist shows Jesus as revealing the mercy of God, in particular in his unique parables such as the Prodigal Son (15:11–32) and the Good Samaritan (10:29–37). He portrays Jesus as a friend of the lost and the least, with a habit of eating with the wrong crowd, at the wrong times, in the wrong way. There seems to be a stronger emphasis in Luke on giving up *everything* to follow Jesus, not just the "nets" of your occupation. The disciples fail in many of the same ways as they do in the other Gospels, but Luke is more benign in his portrayal of them, not as blunt as Mark. Jesus seems to expend infinite patience on them, not a bad characteristic for a leader to emulate.

In Luke's Gospel, before Jesus embarks on his public ministry, he has to overcome a very fundamental problem, in the form of temptations to distort the mission. This episode in Luke, to which Matthew and Mark also attest, and which is also referred to in Hebrews (2:14-18, 4:15), is well worth the attention of Catholic leaders in education since we are also tempted to distort the mission, whether by the lure of "success" in narrow, measurable terms, or by our own motivations for seeking leadership positions for the sake of power and status. It is reassuring to know that Jesus struggled with the same temptations. He was hugely gifted, after all: he could hold an audience with his personal authority and charisma and was capable of "deeds of power" (Acts 2:22) – what we would now call miracles. He clearly felt some stirrings of ego to use those gifts in more worldly ways, perhaps to deliver a worldly kingdom in Israel free from Roman occupation. The American Catholic scripture scholar Luke Timothy Johnson, writing about the temptations, concludes that "the tests would suggest to the Hellenistic reader the threefold categories of vice: love of pleasure, love of possessions, love of glory. Jesus' refusal of these lures would identify him as a righteous person, a sage truly capable of teaching virtue."[7]

Johnson dwells on the third test as having particular significance. In that test, the voice of temptation is chipping away at a relationship which is fundamental to Jesus' identity and sense of mission: his intimate relationship with Abba, his Father. The devil invites Jesus to test his Sonship against the promise of God to protect him: "If you are the Son of God, throw yourself down from here, for it is written, 'He will command his angels concerning you, to protect you'" (Luke 4:9–10). But Jesus will not force his Father's hand. Like everybody else, he will be one who "walks in darkness… yet trusts in the name of the Lord" (Isaiah 50:10) so that "from a subsequent high place he can cry out while leaping, this time with his own choice of words from the Psalm [31:5], 'Father, into your hands I commend my spirit'".[8] In that way he is showing a more perfect trust and dependence on the will of his Father. Johnson describes the inner turmoil of the temptations as a "fundamental battle of the heart",[9] and the reader is invited to understand that everything subsequent to them is a "mopping up operation".[10] Following the victory over temptation, Jesus is seen as a true minister of God's kingdom, so that in all he does, "God [is] with him" (Acts 10:38). He has worked out his mission: not to outdo the world in power and prestige, but to invite people into communion with a loving God through the "narrow door" (Luke 13:24) of simplicity and loving self-emptying.

On the Road

Jesus now embarks on this mission and it very quickly propels him on to the road, shortly after his own folk tried to propel him from the top of a cliff. His message did not go down well in Nazareth, where he was brought up. Scholars reckon that the Nazareth of Jesus' time probably had a population of around 200. This was provincial, agrarian life first-century style: hand to mouth, tightly knit, claustrophobic. Your identity was fixed according to your birth and occupation, and Jesus was believed to be "Joseph's son" (4:22), and his trade, according to Mark, was *tekton* (6:3). We have mostly translated this as carpenter, but the word might be better translated, according to scholars, as craftsman, a worker in wood and stone. So if Joseph and Jesus had a white van it might have said *General Builders* on the side. As such, they probably didn't own land and would have been quite far down the hierarchical structures of society.

So *Yeshua*, still unmarried at the age of thirty, unusual in those days, was not a prophet, he was the village builder, no doubt well respected for his work but not for his sermons. The villagers were scandalised by his change of career when he stood up in the synagogue in Nazareth and read from the scroll that he was going to bring the Gospel (*evangelion*, the Good News) to the poor. They actually wanted to kill him, such was their rage at this affront to their understanding of themselves. With Luke's beautiful sense of structure, it is only later on, in another hilltop moment, that Jesus' sense of identity is affirmed when he hears the voice of his Father saying, "This is my Son, my chosen; listen to him" (9:35). This prophet was accepted by his heavenly Father but rejected by his earthly kin, and he took that hurt with him on the road. There are signs of reconciliation with his family later in Luke, but not in Mark's Gospel, where the relationship with the family remained problematic.

Jesus was on a mission and he did not settle even in places that were sympathetic to his message, such as Capernaum. They wanted to cling to him but he had to go: "I must proclaim the good news of the kingdom of God to the other cities also; for I was sent for this purpose" (Luke 4:43). And what was the nature of this kingdom? What were the values at the heart of this preaching? The scripture scholar John P. Meier sums it up as follows: "At the heart of Jesus' 'good news' is the proclamation that the divine king delights in revealing himself as a loving father, a father who rejoices over regaining his lost children (e.g. the core material behind Luke 15:1–32)."[11] The kingdom was not a place but a dispensation or "reign" as some scholars say, the "reign of God". Luke deliberately positions the ministry of Jesus in the context of world events. Jesus is born during the reign of Augustus, who was revered in the ancient world as the bringer of peace, the saviour of the world. The great irony is that it's the builder from Nazareth who will save the world, not the mighty Augustus. The point is more important than ever in our times: there is another way, another path to peace and salvation, which is quite different to the path of the world.

Change Your Mind

In the synoptic Gospels the way into this kingdom is to "repent" and believe the Good News. In my Catholic upbringing I always assumed that to repent meant to be sorry for my sins, something that could be negotiated in the confessional. I said I was sorry, I was absolved, I did my (not very demanding) penance, I was shriven, job done. Until the next time. But the word used in the Greek to describe what

Jesus was calling for is *metanoia* (Luke 13:5), which is more like change your mind, or your outlook. Or, in our terms, *change your value system*. Jesus spoke in Aramaic, but when the Gospel writers came to choose the Greek word for the community's memory of this primary message of Jesus, that was the word they felt best described the intent.

Thomas Keating, the American Trappist monk, puts it in an even more compelling way when he says, "To repent is not to take on afflictive penances like fasting, vigils, flagellation, or whatever else appeals to your generosity. It means to *change the direction in which you are looking for happiness*."[12] This is the kind of message which will resonate with young people who are looking for happiness and meaning. They have looked in the usual places where the world tells them happiness can be found. Jesus tells them to look in different places, to see reality in a new way. How does Jesus encourage people to do this? By shouting at them from the pulpit, threatening them, bribing them with a lovely afterlife? The teaching method Jesus used most to get people to change their perception of reality was the parable: simple, accessible, memorable *stories*.

I know many people in the Catholic Church who like certainty and rules, and for some, that is their attraction to the Church. There is comfort in having an answer to every dilemma that life throws our way, fixed ethical norms by which one can live a virtuous life. But that is not entirely the legacy of Jesus. Much of his teaching was in the form of parables, a well-known and flexible method of wisdom teaching in the ancient world. John the Baptist seemed to prefer the more direct approach, laying it on the line with some

urgency. Jesus, despite all he learned from the Baptist, used a different pedagogy. James Martin, the American Jesuit priest and author, says that while a definition closes down thought and can be shallow, "a story opens the hearer's mind and is endlessly deep".[13] If God chose to reveal himself so much in this way, then it tells us something important about the nature of God. In a striking formulation, Martin says: "In a sense, Jesus of Nazareth was a story told by God. As Jesus communicated spiritual truths through parables, you might posit the same about God the Father. In order to communicate an essential truth, God offered us a parable: Jesus. Jesus is the parable of God. So for the Christian, if you want to learn more about God, get to know Jesus."[14]

And the parable of God was not a comforting bedside tale. As Meier says, "Far from pleasant stories, Jesus' parables were at times violent verbal attacks on the whole religious world presumed by his audience. They promised a radical reversal of values, bringing in a new world, in a revolution wrought by God, not humans."[15] So to get close to the values of Jesus, of God, we need to include the parables in our reckoning. Some would restrict the search for the values of Jesus to the Sermon on the Mount, especially the Beatitudes. Indeed, the Catechism of the Catholic Church holds a special place for the Sermon on the Mount (Matthew's version). However, if that is the only place you look for the values of Jesus, then you miss out not only the parables but the key encounters Jesus had with people which tell us so much about the nature of God and his pastoral strategy for dealing with the mess and muddle of human lives. Fr Adrian Porter, an English Jesuit priest, makes the point in the reflections at the end of this chapter that so many of the parables are human, not religious. It is the most effective way Jesus found to tell us about God's way, how he regards us and how we should regard one another.

The Face of Mercy

At the beginning of Chapter 15 in Luke's Gospel, two very different groups were "coming near" (Luke 15:1) to Jesus for different reasons. The tax collectors and sinners wanted to "listen to him" (15:1) – they were becoming disciples – while the Pharisees and scribes were grumbling because "This fellow welcomes sinners and eats with them" (15:2). Jesus did not confront their opposition to his mission strategy with a full-frontal assault the way John the Baptist might have done. No, instead "he told them this parable" (15:3) and then proceeded to deliver three of the most memorable parables in the Gospels on the mercy of God: the parables of the lost sheep, the lost coin and the lost son. Pope Francis singles out these parables for special mention in *Misericordiae Vultus*, the Bull of Indiction of the Extraordinary Jubilee of Mercy. He says: "In these parables, God is always presented as full of joy, especially when he pardons. In them, we find the core of the Gospel and of our faith, because mercy is presented as a force that overcomes everything, filling the heart with love and bringing consolation through pardon."[16]

If these parables are the core of the Gospel, then the tale of the lost son, which is unique to Luke, is where this core message finds its richest expression. The bare details of the story are familiar enough: an impatient young man wants his inheritance early, goes to a far country and squanders it all, sinks to the level of the pigs, comes to his senses, rehearses a speech to his father to take him back as a hired hand and sets off home. The father, meanwhile, is not waiting with his arms crossed for the son to come crawling home begging for forgiveness. In one of the most moving moments in the Gospels, Luke reports that while the returning son was still far off, his father saw him, as if he'd been looking out for him, and was "filled with compassion" (Luke 15:20). Not only that, but he abandoned any sense of patriarchal dignity and "ran and put his arms around him and kissed him" (15:20) James Martin SJ, commenting on Luke's use of the word "compassion" says that "the Greek word is the wonderful *esplagchnisthe*, he felt it in his guts – the seat of the feelings in the Hellenistic world."[17]

Many commentators have pointed out that the father bestows the lavish blessings of forgiveness on his son before he has finished his carefully crafted (and crafty) speech of repentance. Throughout the Gospels, especially in the invitations to table, forgiveness is not used as a pre-condition of fellowship (see Zacchaeus, Luke 19:1–10). Forgiveness is given anyway, and that is what releases people to show great love (see Woman at House of Simon the Pharisee, Luke 7:36–50). In the story of the lost son, Jesus presents God the Father not only as forgiving, but as cramping in his gut with compassion at the pitiful state of wayward humanity. The same powerful Greek word is used by Luke to describe Jesus' response to the widow of Nain who is about to bury her only son (Luke 7:13) and the reaction of the Good Samaritan when he discovered the badly beaten man on the side of the road (Luke

10:33). This might explain why Pope Francis, when describing the mercy of God, says that "it is hardly an exaggeration to say that this is a 'visceral' love."[18] We are called to respond to wounded humanity in the same way: not only with pity but with action.

In the ending of all three parables of mercy in Luke Chapter 15 there is an implied contrast between the lavish parties to celebrate the "found" and the grumbling approach of the Pharisees who would exclude sinners from the banquet. The elder son is seen in the same light as the Pharisees, fuming outside while the party goes on inside. He has in fact excluded himself with his lack of forgiveness for his brother. Consider this parable as an exemplum for leaders. Where do we see ourselves in this parable? Perhaps most head teachers or principals see themselves in the role of the dutiful son or daughter who struggles with the magnanimity of God's mercy. It is easier to exclude from the community than to welcome back in the lost ones who have strayed far from what we regard as acceptable. I know this all too well from my own experience, having excluded a number of young people from schools over the years. I could not find a way to let them back in. I fell short of the mercy of the father. Perhaps I was a "slave" to a narrow view of my role and could not see beyond the egregious behaviour of the prodigal. Like the elder son, I would have grumbled that it's not "fair" to treat this lost sheep with such lavish mercy.

Luke Timothy Johnson concludes that in the final scene, the self-isolating elder son standing outside the raucous banquet of God's mercy is a commentary on the Pharisees: "They, like the elder son, had stayed within the covenant and had not wandered off; they had never broken any of the commandments. But (the story suggests) they regarded themselves not as sons but as slaves."[19] Being "good" or dutiful in the narrow sense is not always the Gospel way, seems to be the message. This reign of God is constantly confounding our expectations, reversing our values, demanding more. Part of the journey of Catholic leadership is to honestly acknowledge our own position in these challenging stories: we may have started off in our younger days as the wild prodigal and in leadership have grown into the dutiful elder son or daughter, but what are the prospects of us growing into the father or mother who is able to take the first step towards forgiveness with such disregard for our status?

Where is Your Treasure?

Status and wealth in the ancient world, much like today, went hand in hand, and Jesus was not interested in either. Luke describes the Pharisees as "lovers of money" (16:14) and is the most adamant of all the Gospel writers that attachment to wealth is not compatible with life in the kingdom of God. The parable of the rich fool is prompted by somebody in the crowd asking Jesus to help sort out his inheritance dispute. Jesus replies in the way the crowds would have expected, with a story. In this story we're presented with a rich man who doesn't seem to do much wrong. His land produced abundantly and he decided to build bigger barns to store the excess and in the meantime tells himself to "relax, eat, drink and be merry" (Luke 12:19). This is no more than good capitalist strategy which many of us would sign up to: put something away for a rainy day and don't forget to enjoy yourself in the meantime. But God's response to this very modern attitude is strong: "You fool! This very night your life is being demanded of you. And the things you have prepared, whose will they be?" (Luke 12:20). He has stored up the wrong kind of treasure.

Likewise in the story of the rich ruler, or rich young man in Mark's version. There is a great poignancy to this story since the rich man in this case asks Jesus how to inherit eternal life. Jesus begins by advising him to keep the commandments, in a further reminder that he has come not to abolish the law, but to expand the demand. The rich ruler keeps the commandments, but Jesus asks for more. In this kingdom of God, wealth is seen as an obstacle to following Jesus on his path to communion with the Father. He tells the rich man: "sell all that you own and distribute the money to the poor, and you will have treasure in heaven; then come, follow me" (Luke 18:22). In Mark's Gospel, the rich young man goes away sad since he cannot let go of his wealth, but the scripture scholar Pheme Perkins points out that "Luke omits the reference to the man leaving so that he remains among the audience for Jesus' words about the difficulty rich persons have in entering the kingdom."[20] So, with the rich ruler presumably still within earshot, Jesus, with his love of hyperbole (literally "throwing above", exaggeration), says that it is "easier for a camel to go through the eye of a needle than for someone who is rich to enter the kingdom of God" (Luke 18:25). And he means the kingdom of God in this life, since it is "among you" (Luke 17:21).

If we're honest, we've struggled with this one from

the beginning. The Church has not hesitated for much of its history to accumulate wealth, as have many of its members. In the West today more people are more materially comfortable than at any other time in history. The young people in our schools and colleges are brought up in a covetous culture, where happiness and status are dependent on acquiring the consumer goods of choice. I haven't heard any commentator saying that Jesus considers poverty to be a good thing. He is critical of a system which impoverishes people, and we'll see in the next chapter how he holds up for praise the man who resists the system. Poverty is destructive of human dignity, not a state to aspire to. The message in Luke's Gospel seems to be that if wealth is our god, if material gain is our primary motivation in life, then there's no space for God. In the parable of the sower, the seed that fell among thorns represents "the ones who hear; but as they go on their way, they are choked by the cares and riches and pleasures of life, and their fruit does not mature" (Luke 8:14).

In my experience, young people are very open to this message. They are assailed from all angles by smart messages about brand acquisition and body perfection. This can lead to states of high anxiety, as we saw in Chapter 1, but there is still somewhere in their young hearts a latent idealism which responds to the Gospel message of simplicity and service. After all, you will never have enough to satisfy a covetous heart. They are open to hearing Jesus say to them "do not worry about your life, what you will eat, or about your body, what you will wear" (Luke 12:22). In the value system of Jesus, it's all about what your treasure is, what the most important thing for you is. At the end of the passage on worry, Jesus concludes, "where your treasure is, there your heart will be also" (Luke 12:34). I've heard many people misread this as where you heart is, there will your treasure be, but that's not the point. Jesus is saying, show me your treasure and I'll show you the state of your heart. It's a question for every disciple to ask, but for our purposes it's a question for every educational community to ask: where is our treasure? That will determine everything.

Abba, Father

Jesus' treasure was his relationship with his Father. Many scholars emphasise what they call the "Abba-experience" as a major source of the mission confidence of Jesus. Meier comments that Jesus "taught his disciples to imitate his intimate relationship to God as Abba. From this total confidence in and abandonment to God as Father sprang Jesus' startling praxis and teaching."[21] Jesus did not teach his disciples to pray systematically from the beginning of their mission. Jesus was often described as going off to pray alone, especially in Luke, where he would "withdraw to deserted places and pray" (Luke 5:16). Before big decisions, like the choosing of the twelve, "he spent the night in prayer to God" (Luke 6:12). It seems that the disciples had to ask Jesus to teach them how to pray, with the goad that John the Baptist taught *his* disciples (Luke 11:1). The "Father prayer" which followed, according to Meier, is "usually held to be fairly close to what Jesus taught his disciples"[22] – the actual words from the very mouth of Jesus, translated into Greek. In Luke's Gospel, Jesus begins his prayer with the direct "Father" (11:2) (as opposed to the more formal

address in Matthew, "Our Father" [6:9]), which probably reflects the emphatic Aramaic address, *Abba*. We are invited into a conversation with God, our compassionate Father, who longs to come running over the fields towards us.

Perhaps the most dramatic prayer experience in Luke's Gospel is the transfiguration. In that scene, Jesus takes his inner circle of Peter, James and John (I wonder how the others felt on those occasions?) up the mountain "to pray" (Luke 9:28). The clue as to what might have been in Jesus' heart at this time is provided earlier in the chapter when Jesus is praying with the disciples near him and he asks them, "Who do the crowds say that I am?" (Luke 9:18). This is a question which many leaders will relate to: how am I regarded by this community? Who do they think I am? On the mountain, Jesus prays for the answer, "and while he was praying, the appearance of his face changed" (9:29). What has happened? Luke tells us that Jesus has received his answer. The voice of his Father declares, "This is my Son, my Chosen; listen to him" (9:35). In this mystical experience, Jesus is made radiant by the affirming love of his Father. He now has strength in his identity and mission, and from that point on "he set his face to go to Jerusalem" (9:51).

Jesus prayed because this was how he could encounter his Father directly and personally and grow in union with him. This has been true ever since. To experience any kind of friendship (intimacy) with God, there are certain conditions attested by the tradition: solitude, silence, simplicity of heart and a daily practice, or *ascesis*. Any community which follows Jesus, therefore, should have prayer at its heart. In the Acts of the Apostles, Luke says that the early Christian communities "devoted themselves to the apostles' teaching and fellowship, to the breaking of bread and the prayers" (Acts 2:42). To grow in the friendship of God is a definition of the Christian life which appeals to young people and makes sense to adults. If we keep the purpose of our schools only on the level of the intellect (definitions, characteristics, research findings), then we will lack what Gerald Grace calls "mission integrity" (see "Reflections by Leaders in Catholic Education", Chapter 5) and our commitment will have no roots. If we are growing in prayerful encounter with the God of love and compassion, then we are leading our faith community by example.

This is My Body

Leading by example was a feature of the life of Jesus. He revealed the kingdom, or way of God, to us in his parables, in his encounters with sinners, in his courageous engagement with the authorities of his day, in his miracles, but perhaps above all in his death, which showed the full extent of his self-emptying (kenosis). On the night he was betrayed he reminded us that he had given us his body, not just in the last supper, but from the moment of his conception. James Martin SJ came to this insight while saying Mass: "When I lifted up the host, I realised that Jesus took his body to so many places; he *gave* his body to people, physically. He *brought* himself to people – saying, in essence, 'This is my body. Here I am.' It helped me think of the familiar words 'This is my body' in a new light."[23] This extraordinary generosity of God is witnessed in the nature of the death of Jesus. As Raymond Brown, the American scripture scholar,

comments in his recorded talks on the origins of the Johannine community,[24] Jesus could have died of a disease in a small town in Galilee and still have been raised to glory by God, but that is not what happened.

God had given his body to the human race in the form of Jesus in a profound act of solidarity. God took on the full extent of the human condition and saw life from our point of view. Vatican II's Pastoral Constitution on the Church in the Modern World, *Gaudium et Spes*, puts it this way: "For by his incarnation the Son of God united himself in some sense with every human being. He laboured with human hands, thought with a human mind, acted with a human will, and loved with a human heart."[25] And this was not a "safe" conditional giving, with Jesus protected from the worst excesses of the human condition. On the contrary, Jesus experienced not only the warmth of friendship, the pleasures of nature, the satisfaction of a job well done in wood or stone, but also the mockery and cruelty of people at their worst. Jesus could easily have slipped away that evening after the last supper, but he stayed, and when the guards came "they seized him and led him away" (Luke 22:54). The grammar changes from active to passive: the driven, inspirational preacher and healer who had covered so many miles in his mission is now taken and led.

He does not turn his encounter with the human condition into a battle, for human beings to understand the message of God by domination. That temptation has already been faced and rejected. Instead, he absorbs the full force of men's violence and in his moment of greatest powerlessness, fixed by nails to a six-foot upright beam and cross-beam (*patibulum*), dying dreadfully from blood loss and asphyxiation, mocked by the onlooking crowd, he utters a prayer of forgiveness: "Father, forgive them; for they do not know what they are doing" (Luke 23:34). He prays for those who persecute him. There must be something essential in the *type* of death Jesus suffered which tells us about the nature of God. The abject nature of the death, one in which he has been humiliated and killed by human beings at their most violent, tells us that there is something about powerlessness which is fundamental to our understanding of the truth. Jesus interrupts the human condition at that point and says: your normal ways of power and violence in order to secure the status of your tribe, your nation, are not the ways of God. Jesus, the vulnerable name for God, shows us another way: non-violent, forgiving, self-emptying.

In his rising from the dead, the violence and pain are transformed and God declares universal peace and reconciliation. The mysterious risen body of Jesus bears the wounds of his passion (as well as any other wounds or scars he picked up along the way), but his heart bears no trace of bitterness towards either the men who killed him or the friends who denied and deserted him in the hour of crisis. In fact, the biggest denier is invited to become the leader of the community who will spread this message of forgiveness and reconciliation to the ends of the earth. It's no wonder that the disciples at the end of Luke's Gospel "returned to Jerusalem with great joy" (24:52). They had met their risen Lord on the road to Emmaus. He had appeared to them in the locked upper room and his first words were, "Peace be with you" (24:36). There is no anger in the Risen Jesus. He sends his Spirit to the community and they are

fired with zeal for this message. Jesus has reconciled the human race to God and his followers are called to the "ministry of reconciliation" (2 Corinthians 5:18), appealing to the world on behalf of Christ: "be reconciled to God" (2 Corinthians 5:20).

The reign of God began with the life and death of Jesus and we continue his mission with the inspiration of his Spirit. There is work to be done as we can plainly see. Much of the world carries on as it has always done: status and wealth are held in esteem, violence is used against individuals or groups in order to dominate and control. Injustice and corruption are widespread. There is goodness too, of course, and many people who have no interest in Christianity lead good and fruitful lives in the service of others. Vatican II reminded us that the Spirit is active in all people of goodwill, but for the Christian, and any community which calls itself Christian, the inspiration and motivation to follow a loving path comes from the Gospel. This is not an abstract and difficult message, nor is it half-hearted. Richard Rohr, in his daily meditations, described the reign of God as being all about "the grace-driven, love-driven transformation of the self and the world".[26] This is the message we're invited to put in front of our young people.

In the next chapter we will turn our attention back to our schools and colleges and attempt to establish the values of Jesus, Gospel values, what he stood for and died for, in the hope that we might draw closer in our day-to-day community life to the way of Jesus, the kingdom of God. In this briefest of surveys of Luke's Gospel (for more detailed and scholarly work on the Gospels, see the further reading section at the end of this chapter) we have encountered a unique historical figure: Yeshua, the first-century provincial Jew whom we believe is "true God and true man",[27] the revelation of the truth of reality. If we were to draw up a list of adjectives to describe Jesus in Luke's Gospel we might end up with something like: observant, practical, quick-witted, clever, imaginative, humorous, humble, earthy, authoritative, driven, passionate, prayerful, brave, honest, loyal, compassionate, kind, forgiving, joyful, loving, generous, Spirit-led, prophetic. This is what a Gospel-inspired person looks like, and it gives us a good starting point for describing a Gospel-inspired school.

Reflections by Leaders in Catholic Education

Most of the Catholic leaders spoke about the counter-cultural message of the Gospel and the tensions of running a school which holds those values in esteem. They cited examples of the very high demand in the Gospels for forgiveness and the difficulty of dealing with young people who break the community's rules. The counter-cultural message is also felt keenly with the emphasis of Jesus on simplicity and non-attachment to wealth. My reading of some of this anxiety is that it was probably easier for priests and religious who had taken vows of poverty to speak with authority on this issue. For a lay leadership, with many of the status symbols associated with worldly success, it is harder to preach simplicity. There was a general appetite among the head teachers for more formation in the scriptures. Those with an RE background may have studied theology and scripture, but for most this is very much an area in which support and training is needed so that leaders can go

beyond a list of Gospel values to reflect for themselves on the texts with some depth and discernment. Then head teachers will be able to open up the richness of the Gospel to students and staff.

ॐ

I think people assume that what is in the Gospels is highly religious, and some of it is, especially in John's Gospel, but once you actually read the Gospel and you start looking at the kind of parables or sermons or miracles or whatever, once you start looking at these, very often they're very, very human. If you read the Gospels, especially read through a whole Gospel, and you discard the narrative part, you very rapidly begin to see what those values are. So you'll have these parables which are saying something very clearly about human life, human interaction, and it seems to be that's where the values come from because it's Jesus saying, "This is the way that you're called to deal with your fellow human beings." I think what schools need to do is to focus on those, quite literally, taking the text, which might be just five or six lines long, sitting down with it maybe once a year, looking at it and saying to staff, "Does our practice of forgiveness in this school reflect the instruction of Jesus to forgive 70 × 7 times?" That's not to be naïve and it's a balance with justice and the practicalities of running a big school but at the same time, is there serious forgiveness in this school or is it something a bit different?

—Adrian Porter, Delegate for Education for the British Province of the Society of Jesus

Every single one of our learners, to one extent or another, has an elevated level of anxiety all the time. So when a new member of staff comes to us I'll describe it like that feeling you get when you're about to sit an exam or have a driving test, that level of raised adrenalin and anxiety that's there all the time before you sit that test. For most of our learners they are at that level as a base, they're always at that level because everything around them just doesn't quite fit. So we'll see, at the extreme end, quite dangerous behaviour from somebody who's essentially frightened because they can't communicate with us. About 40% of our learners are non-verbal, not because they have a physical impairment but because the cognitive connections that make communication possible are a dysfunction with them. So they're unable to communicate, I would say, in our language.

—Annie Sutton, Executive Principal, St Joseph's Special School, Cranleigh

To the Church generally I think Pope Francis has been a wonderful witness of someone living out Gospel values, the way that he has gone out and washed the feet of people in prison, washed the feet of Muslim people. That kind of thing is really powerful, and shows he's a person of the people, he behaves in the way I imagine Jesus would have behaved. He does show that merciful face, merciful like the Father. He looks like he loves everyone and would give everyone a second chance. I love the way that he will just go out into the streets. We've got a friend who's a

Swiss Guard and they say he's terrible to keep an eye on because he'll pop out and they won't know where he is. I think that's fantastic and people love that. Friends who are not Catholic, not even Christian, think that Pope Francis is really cool. My teenage girls and their friends are all following him on Snap Chat and Instagram, even the ones who are not Catholic. He must be having a very powerful effect.

—Sarah Conrad, Head of Prep School, St Teresa's, Effingham

I keep directing you back to *The Catholic School* document of 1977. I have read them all in detail. This one is the most inspirational of anything that's ever come out of Rome and I really do believe that every school leader ought to have a copy on his or her desk. It's beautifully written because it balances realism (the people who wrote it were realists) with idealism, they've put the two together. That's extremely helpful. Also, they showed remarkably perceptive analysis of the signs of the times, what was developing in the late 1970s and was going to come to full flowering in the 1980s was the globalisation and marketisation of the world, fuelled by a strong ideology of individual possession of enjoyment, of self-regard. They recognised that in 1977 and warned Catholic educators that they must be preparing their counter-cultural message against what was a global powerful ideology. We have to be resolute in our attempts to be counter-cultural against these wider, what can almost be called corrupting, influences of the wider society in which individual celebrity success, possession, technology, immediate gratifying sensation, these are the things that are strong in this globalised country. Our job is to resist that. To put out alternative models, to give alternative visions of what life could be like.

—Gerald Grace, Director of the Centre for Research and Development in Catholic Education, St Mary's, Twickenham

I think there are clearly elements of Christianity which have gone very deep into the culture, and certain values, even British values, I think must have their roots, to some extent, in Christianity. But there is, I think, a powerful counter-cultural message at work in all sorts of ideas in the Gospels. I think the whole idea of an afterlife, resurrection, really fundamental things, the person of Christ, the identity of Christ, love of enemies, and the whole question of wealth and poverty. It's very interesting doing the story of the Rich Young Man, for example, which I've taught in every school I've been in. Or to talk about luxury and absolute poverty and how they can co-exist or not and whether there's a moral imperative on those people living in luxury to give to those people who have nothing. I think that's incredibly challenging.

—Hugh Walters, Head of Theology, Downside School, Stratton-on-the-Fosse

I think it's getting across the idea that these are the boundaries to the values. You find some interpretations that say that being a Christian is just about being nice to people.

We water it down so far so that we don't offend anybody but some of the values, if you read the Gospels, they are challenging. It's not about being nice to people, it's about challenging society and caring for the poor, the vulnerable, and making a difference and not just saying things are OK; if we're all just nice to people, it'll all be OK. I think it's getting that balance, about having values which are challenging and having an institution that can reflect that challenge, can accept that challenge and be challenged.

—Dr Ann Casson, Research Fellow at National Institute for Christian Education Research (NICER), Canterbury Christ Church University

What we have always tried to produce is young people who will work for the common good, who will work for the good of others. We have tried to have a view of education which says that the reason for your talents and gifts is not for yourself but for others and you're called to live for others. That is a very powerful philosophy that we instil in our young people. It's also something that even those children that we take in our schools who are not Catholic [are taught], to try and help them understand that what they're called to do is live for others. It has to be, I think, a good thing.

—Diocesan Officer, Catholic Diocesan Education Department

I actually think the Gospel message is quite hard-hitting, and even if you put it down to its most basic of "love God and love neighbour", what does "love God" mean? Love God means to be in a relationship with God. So, if you want to know God, if you want to love God, it's got to be underpinned with prayer, it's got to be underpinned with silence and with listening and with discernment. We've got to try, as much as we can, and we're only human, to put God first. Ideally you're abandoning your own will to the will of God and that again is quite grandiose phrasing for something which is really very difficult to do, I think. So you can say, "I'm going to abandon my will to God" and almost immediately something else gets in the way because you say that "I have to take account of my family" or "I have to take account of my career" or "I have to take account of the needs of the community around me" and so actually the will of God within that may be blurred.

—Charlotte Cummins, Senior Deputy Head, Prior Park College, Bath

Reflections from Scripture

His divine power has given us everything needed for life and godliness, through the knowledge of him who called us by his own glory and goodness. Thus he has given us, through these things, his precious and very great promises, so that through them you may escape from the corruption that is in the world because of lust, and may become participants of the divine nature. For this very reason, you must make every effort to support your faith with goodness, and goodness with knowledge, and knowledge with self-control, and self-control with endurance, and endurance with godliness, and godliness with mutual affection, and mutual affection with love. For if these things are yours and are increasing among you, they keep you from being ineffective and unfruitful in the knowledge of our Lord Jesus Christ. (2 Peter 1:3–8)

He said to his disciples, "Therefore I tell you, do not worry about your life, what you will eat, or about your body, what you will wear. For life is more than food, and the body more than clothing. Consider the ravens: they neither sow nor reap, they have neither storehouse nor barn, and yet God feeds them. Of how much more value are you than the birds! And can any of you by worrying add a single hour to your span of life? If then you are not able to do so small a thing as that, why do you worry about the rest? Consider the lilies, how they grow; they neither toil nor spin; yet I tell you, even Solomon in all his glory was not clothed like one of these. But if God so clothes the grass of the field, which is alive today and tomorrow is thrown into the oven, how much more will he clothe you – you of little faith! And do not keep striving for what you are to eat and what you are to drink, and do not keep worrying. For it is the nations of the world that strive after all these things, and your Father knows that you need them. Instead, strive for his kingdom, and these things will be given to you as well.

Do not be afraid, little flock, for it is your Father's good pleasure to give you the kingdom. Sell your possessions, and give alms. Make purses for yourselves that do not wear out, an unfailing treasure in heaven, where no thief comes near and no moth destroys. For where your treasure is, there your heart will be also." (Luke 12:22–34)

Suggestions for Further Reading

Raymond E. Brown SS, Joseph A. Fitzmyer SJ, Roland E. Murphy, O.Carm. (editors), *The New Jerome Biblical Commentary* (London: Burns and Oates, 1990). A commentary on every book of the Bible, along with essays on key themes, written by the significant figures of twentieth-century Catholic biblical scholarship.

James Martin SJ, *Jesus: A Pilgrimage*, 16-CD audiobook (New York: Harper Audio, 2015). Audiobooks have been a recent discovery for me. I have heard many great books on scripture and spirituality in my car, making otherwise tedious journeys richly rewarding. James Martin's book on Jesus is a highly engaging blend of travelogue in the Holy Land, personal biography, scripture scholarship and spirituality.

Denis McBride, C.Ss.R., *The Parables of Jesus* (Chawton: Redemptorist Publications, 1999). If you want to concentrate on the parables, then Denis McBride's book will provide a compelling reading of these Gospel stories as subversive texts of the kingdom.

Pheme Perkins, *Reading the New Testament: An Introduction* (Mahwah, NJ: Paulist Press, 2012). An excellent introduction to all the books of the New Testament written in a highly informative and readable manner.

Luke Timothy Johnson, *Sacra Pagina: The Gospel of Luke* (Minnesota: Liturgical Press, 1991). If you want to focus on one Gospel at a time, then the *Sacra Pagina* series is highly recommended. James Martin makes frequent reference to the work of Luke Timothy Johnson in *Jesus: A Pilgrimage*.

CHAPTER 3

Gospel Values for Schools: a reading of Luke

– CHAPTER 3 –

Gospel Values for Schools: a reading of Luke

Any mission review in our schools could fruitfully begin with the question we looked at in the previous chapter, "Where is your treasure?" When you take an honest look at your school and ask yourself candidly what your time and money is spent on (the best indicator of your actual priorities), you may be close to answering the question. We can say what we like about our mission, but it's what we *actually* do, or don't do, day in and day out that defines our mission. To help school leaders to evaluate their mission I have identified ten Gospel values drawn from the Gospel of Luke. I have tried to do what Bishop Stock suggested we should do in *Christ at the Centre* when he said that "these Gospel values need to be explicitly named, their meaning unpacked and pupils helped to understand how they relate to their lives at school".[1] My list of ten is not identical to Bishop Stock's but it is very close.

Whatever set of Gospel values you adopt for your school, it is important that they do not just become a leadership exercise conducted on a staff training day at the beginning of term and once the daily grind kicks in, all talk of "values" is quickly forgotten. The point is that "rooted in the teaching of Christ, these Gospel values should constitute the targets and outcomes of the educational enterprise in every

Catholic school".[2] They should be written into the foundation documents, such as the mission statement and school development plan, and used as the measure by which to evaluate practice and make key decisions. For each of the ten values there is a brief commentary on examples from Luke's Gospel, followed by some questions designed to help school leaders to reflect on their current practice, and then suggestions for exemplars of the values.

Gospel Value no. 1 – Compassion
kindness, service of neighbour

Pope Francis reminds us in *Misericordiae Vultus* that Pope Paul VI in his closing address to the Vatican Council in 1965 said that "charity has been the principal religious feature of this Council… the old story of the Good Samaritan has been the model of the spirituality of the Council." He continues by saying that "a wave of affection and admiration flowed from the Council over the modern world of humanity… Another point we must stress is this: all this rich teaching is channelled in one direction, the service of mankind, of every condition, in every weakness and need."[3] The emphasis of Pope Francis on the mercy of God finds its modern roots in the

Vatican Council, summed up in those powerful statements at the beginning and the end of the Council from John XXIII and Paul VI. In the address by Paul VI, the priority of the Church is again made clear: service of people, especially in need. It is the kind of message that young people are likely to take at face value. Perhaps that's why Jesus introduced into his discourses the striking novelty of behaving like a child.

The parable of the good Samaritan, like so many others, is prompted by a tricky situation. A lawyer has stood up and asked Jesus a question "to test Jesus" (Luke 10:25). He wants to know how to inherit eternal life. Another trap. Jesus is mentally agile in these situations, quick-thinking. He invites the lawyer to answer his own question (Jesus very rarely answers a question directly). The lawyer repeats the essence of the law, which is to love God and neighbour, but to justify his loaded question he asks Jesus, "And who is my neighbour?" (10:29). The wrong answer at this point could be very divisive, even dangerous. The answer Jesus comes up with is the story of a man who gets badly beaten up on the road to Jericho, and is left for dead. The first two to come upon him, a priest and a Levite, go out of their way to avoid the problem and pass by "on the other side" (10:31). Luke Timothy Johnson explains that the shock of this parable to its first audience is "the recognition that Jews esteemed for their place in the people and dedicated to holiness before the Lord would allow considerations of personal safety… to justify not even crossing the road to look."[4]

The greater shock is that the hero with the human heart is a despised Samaritan. By not only stopping to check on the injured man but taking him with him to the nearest inn to be cared for, he increased his own vulnerability. Jesus makes it clear that the point of the parable is not that the injured man deserved to be cared for, "but rather the demand to become a person who treats everyone encountered – however frightening, alien, naked or defenceless – with compassion."[5] Jesus may use parables a lot, but sometimes, for the avoidance of doubt, he spells out the meaning, as he does here when he says: "Go and do likewise" (10: 37). The Gospel of God is not just an interesting story, it is a call to act in the face of suffering. Pope Francis has reminded us of this with his call to assist the refugees struggling across Europe. He cuts through the politics, just like Jesus, and says: help them. They are your neighbours. See Christ in them.

Key Quotations from Luke

"If you love those who love you, what credit is that to you? For even sinners love those who love them." (6:32) – The Sermon on the Plain

"When the Lord saw her, he had compassion for her and said to her, 'Do not weep.'" (7:13) – The Widow of Nain

"Which of these three, do you think was a neighbour to the man who fell into the hands of the robbers?" (10:36) – The Good Samaritan

Gospel Values in School

- In what ways are compassion and kindness held in esteem in your school? Are examples of such behaviour from history, from current news and from students in the school praised and highlighted?

- To what extent is service of neighbour promoted in your school, in the form of responses to emergency needs, but also programmes of support for the needy in the community, such as refugees, the elderly or the homeless?

- Is kindness an explicit expectation of the behaviour of the adults in the school as enshrined in the Staff Code of Conduct?

Exemplars of Gospel Values: Compassion

- **Jesuit Refugee Service** – founded in 1980 as a work of the Society of Jesus, the JRS now operates in 50 countries and directly benefits 900,000 people. http://www.jrsuk.net/

- **Mary's Meals** – provides life-changing meals to some of the world's poorest children every day they attend school; 1,101,206 children are now being fed every day. https://www.marysmeals.org.uk

- **Saint Teresa of Calcutta** (1910–97) – an icon of God's mercy to the most vulnerable members of society, especially in India, where she founded the Missionaries of Charity family of Sisters, Brothers, Fathers and Co-Workers. Awarded the Nobel Peace Prize in 1979.

Gospel Value no. 2 – Non-violence
gentleness

Matthew's Gospel has a Sermon on the Mount, which seems to be delivered to the inner group of disciples. Luke's equivalent sermon is delivered "on a level place" (6:17) to a great crowd of disciples. Luke's Beatitudes are shorter than Matthew's and include not just blessings but "woes" against the rich – Matthew's version was the one favoured by the Church for many years. After the Beatitudes, Luke goes straight to the stunningly blunt and counterintuitive exhortation, "love your enemies" (6:27), which has been a challenge for Christians ever since. The Jewish tradition of an "eye for an eye" was a way of limiting retribution and was based on sound social logic: don't let vengeance get out of control. Jesus, however, is asking for more. As Luke Timothy Johnson says, "Luke has Jesus demand of his followers a standard for human relationships that involves a 'going beyond' or more than the norm of reciprocity, of *do ut des*. The 'golden rule' of 'do as you would want done' is not the ultimate norm here but rather, 'do as God would do'."[6]

An example of Jesus' non-violent response to a hostile reception can be found in his encounter with a Samaritan village. As we've seen from the parable above, Jews and Samaritans were historically hostile to each other over a fundamental difference about where God should be worshipped. It was never going to be easy for Jesus to preach in a Samaritan village, and sure enough he was rejected. James and John, the "sons of thunder", want to incinerate the place in an act of divine temper. Even though they are in the "inner circle" of Jesus they are clearly struggling with the core concept of non-violence, as many Christians still do. Jesus "rebuked them" (9:55) for their violent suggestion and moved on. As we've already seen in the arrest and death of Jesus, there was no intention to turn this mission into a battle. God does not promote violence – he wants his followers to be non-violent peace-makers.

Dr Ann Casson points out in her reflections at the end of this chapter that Christians from the very beginning have struggled with the radical demands of Jesus. When our young people ask us to explain the violence of Christians over the centuries (the crusades, papal armies, support for repressive regimes), we need to be honest and avoid the casuistry of "cultural conditioning", and admit that very often we have fallen short of the standards of God. Many in the Christian tradition have risen to the challenge of non-violence, from the first Christian martyrs who refused to serve in the imperial army, to the American social activist Dorothy Day. Walter Wink, the renowned American biblical scholar and advocate of non-violent resistance, comments: "Even where nonviolent resistance was successfully used, it tends to be neglected. A people kept ignorant of the existence of the history of nonviolence will naturally believe that it is impractical and unrealistic."[7] He then provides a remarkable litany of non-violent resistance to oppression and injustice throughout history, noting an exponential increase in recent years which has largely gone unnoticed.

Key Quotations from Luke

"If anyone strikes you on the cheek, offer the other also." (6:29) – Love for Enemies

"'Lord, do you want us to command fire to come down from heaven and consume them?' But he turned and rebuked them." (9:54) – A Samaritan Village Refuses to Receive Jesus

"But Jesus said, "No more of this!" And he touched his ear and healed him." (22:51) – The Betrayal and Arrest of Jesus

Gospel Values in School

- To what extent is the history of non-violent resistance movements celebrated and promoted in your school's curriculum?

- Is your school's attitude to aggressive behaviour, including violent and aggressive language, rooted in the Gospel, and are the consequences clearly set out in the behaviour policy in ways which are developmental and not just punitive?

Exemplars of Gospel Values: Non-Violence

- **Mohandas ("Mahatma") Gandhi** (1869–1948) – the leader of India's independence movement and the architect of a form of non-violent civil disobedience that would influence many subsequent movements.

- **Dorothy Day** (1897–1980) – an American journalist, social activist and Catholic convert. In the 1930s, she founded the Catholic Worker Movement, a pacifist movement that combined direct aid for the poor and homeless with non-violent and direct action on their behalf. Her conversion from a bohemian lifestyle is described in her autobiography, *The Long Loneliness*.

- **Pax Christi** – the International Catholic Peace Movement – founded in 1945 as an international movement of Catholics in Europe who believed in reconciliation at the end of World War II, now a global network committed to peace and justice. http://paxchristi.org.uk/

Gospel Value no. 3 – Justice
action against corruption and oppression

Luke's parable of the ten pounds was often overlooked in favour of Matthew's similar parable of the talents (Matthew 25:14–30). In my Catholic school upbringing, the parable of the talents was always used as an encouragement to use your natural abilities to the full. The "wicked and lazy slave" (Matthew 25:26) was the boy who buried his natural talent for mathematics and chose instead to dream out of the window. That view, as James Martin explains, is based on a misreading of "talents" in the parable: "a *talanton* was a huge amount of money, equivalent to roughly fifteen years' wages, so the man is turning over to his servants a ridiculous amount of wealth."[8] Jesus' use of hyperbole would once more have captured the imagination of his

listeners. The parable is about money, lots of it, and how the three servants respond to being given money to look after while their master is away.

Scholarly interpretations vary concerning the message of these parables in Matthew and Luke. James Martin reports that John Donahue considers the point of the parable to be the lazy servant's timidity. He has been treated fairly and made a victim of himself by refusing to engage with his master. Luke Timothy Johnson, on the other hand, sees Luke's parable in the context of the kingly proclamation of Jesus at the end of Luke's Gospel. In this reading, the servants whose faithful use of possessions is rewarded by authority are none other than the twelve apostles. The ones who do not want this ruler to gain royal power are the leaders of the people who reject Jesus as king. The very fact that two such prominent scholars arrive at such different interpretations of the parable reminds us that much of Jesus' teaching is an invitation to struggle with human stories and try to "read" them in the bigger picture of his Gospel.

Denis McBride, a Redemptorist scripture scholar, arrives at a different meaning again and one which I personally find the most convincing. He begins with the difficulty in identifying Jesus/God with a ruler who does not contradict the third servant's description of him as "a harsh man" (Luke 19:22) and who concludes his business by having his enemies slaughtered in his presence. That is not the God we saw running over the fields with tears of compassion in his eyes in the parable of the lost son. McBride concludes that "the parable's interpretation as a coded critique of rich landowners' abuse of their economic power would seem more consistent with Jesus' own values".[9] In this reading, the third slave is the moral hero due to his non-violent refusal to cooperate with a rapacious and harsh ruler who makes money from the labour of the poor and who makes his money make money while most of the population live in penury and oppression. He is an example of non-violent resistance against an unjust system. Loving your enemy does not mean that you should be passive in the face of aggressive injustice, but nor do you respond with like for like: non-violent action for justice calls for clarity (what's the problem?) and creativity (what's the solution?).

Key Quotations from Luke

"Because this widow keeps bothering me, I will grant her justice." (18:5) – The Parable of the Widow and the Unjust Judge

"You are a harsh man; you take what you did not deposit, and reap what you did not sow." (19:21) – The Parable of the Ten Pounds

"Then he entered the temple and began to drive out those who were selling things there." (19:45) – Jesus Cleanses the Temple

Gospel Values in Action

• Does your school help to develop the students' understanding of injustice in the world – economic or social – and encourage advocacy for change?

• Does your school help to develop the students' understanding of oppression – e.g. sexism and violence against women, or racism – not only in other cultures but in its more subtle manifestations in our society? Is the school strong enough in its response to any sexist or racist language or innuendo, and is this modelled by the staff in their routine discourse?

• What examples of figures from history or the present day who stood against injustice and oppression do you hold up to the community for esteem?

Exemplars of Gospel Values: Justice

• **Martin Luther King** (1929–68) – an American Baptist minister and activist who was a leader in the American civil rights movement, committed to non-violent means to achieve justice and equality. He left us with some of the most inspiring speeches ever delivered.

• **Justice for the 96** – The Hillsborough disaster was a human crush at Hillsborough football stadium in Sheffield on 15 April 1989 which left 96 Liverpool football fans dead and 766 injured. A twenty-seven-year struggle for justice and truth ended on 26 April 2016 when a jury returned a verdict that the supporters were unlawfully killed and were in no way to blame for the disaster.

• **Malala Yousafzai** (b. 1997) – the young girl who advocated education for girls in the north-west area of Pakistan run by the Taliban and was shot in the head on a school bus for refusing to be silent. She was flown to Britain for medical treatment and survived the attack. She went on to become an international advocate for women's and children's right to education. She was awarded the Nobel Peace Prize in 2014.

Gospel Value no. 4 – Integrity
honesty, truth-telling

One of the things I have always admired about Jesus was his outspoken courage. In Luke's Gospel he seems to be permanently engaged in a public row with the Pharisees, a group of lay intellectuals defined in *The New Jerome Biblical Commentary* as the "Separated Ones, probably so dubbed by opponents because of their professed strict avoidance of Gentiles, of unclean persons, of sinners, and of Jews less observant of the Torah".[10] Scholars do make the point that the Pharisees were not all bad, and in fact they may well have been set up as "straw men" by the Gospel writers, convenient representations of an attitude which was at odds with the mission of Jesus. In any case, Jesus consistently attacks any displays of public worth and adulation, especially when it covers a rotten interior. We've seen already how strong the "mission integrity" of Jesus was, arising from a direct, prayerful and transforming relationship with his Father. His inner and his outer life were in complete harmony. The opposite of that, what he called hypocrisy, riled him at times to a passion.

In Luke's Sermon on the Plain the disciples who are fulfilling the mission requirements of Jesus include those who are persecuted for standing up for the Gospel. Jesus says to them, "blessed are you when people hate you, and when they exclude you, revile you, and defame you on account of the Son of Man" (6:22). We have already seen how the mission and message of Jesus was in many ways profoundly counter-cultural. Those who benefited from power and injustice had good reason to be hostile to the message of universal dignity from the *tekton* from Nazareth. His disciples from the very beginning endured opposition and persecution, and still do to the present day. Standing up for the Gospel, even at the risk of personal danger, has always been a feature of the Christian tradition. This again is the kind of message which young people respond to, with their innate sense of integrity. A diocesan officer, in the reflections at the end of this section, reminds us that in the digital age, there is more pressure than ever to conform to the instant opinions generated by social media. For the first time in history, young people occupy the public forum, online.

The early Christians faced many attempts to silence them. In the Acts of the Apostles Luke reports that Peter and John were summoned before the Council of rulers, elders and scribes in Jerusalem, who were worried because the execution of Jesus had not stopped his message spreading. When they asked the disciples by what power they acted, they were amazed at the confident reply of these "uneducated and ordinary men" (Acts 4:13). The authorities were rattled by this new sect and ordered them to "speak no more to anyone in this name" (Acts 4:17). Peter and John were unmoved by the order, not so much out of defiance but because they "cannot keep from speaking about what [they] have seen and heard" (Acts 4:20). In Luke it is the Spirit which gives the disciples such confidence and transforms Peter the denier into Peter the proclaimer. Jesus makes the same point in Luke's Gospel when he tells the disciples not to worry about what to say when they are dragged in front of rulers and authorities, "for the Holy Spirit will teach you at that very hour what you ought to say" (12:12). Fearless integrity and public witness to the truth have always been required of the disciples of Jesus Christ.

Key Quotations from Luke

"Now you Pharisees clean the outside of the cup and of the dish, but inside you are full of greed and wickedness" (11:39) – Jesus Denounces Pharisees and Lawyers

"Do not worry about how you are to defend yourselves or what you are to say; for the Holy Spirit will teach you at that very hour what you ought to say." (12:11-12) – Exhortation to Fearless Confession

"He said to them, "Go and tell that fox [Herod] for me, 'Listen, I am casting out demons and performing cures today and tomorrow, and on the third day I finish my work.'" (13:32) – The Lament over Jerusalem

Gospel Values in Action

- Is integrity and truth-telling explicitly honoured and encouraged in your school's policies?

- Is "mission integrity" evident in the school because the public pronouncements of mission match the daily reality? How is this evaluated?

- Are examples from history and from the present day of prophetic voices who stood up for what is right held in esteem by your school?

Exemplars of Gospel Values: Integrity

- **Dietrich Bonhoeffer** (1906–45) – a German Lutheran pastor, theologian and anti-Nazi dissident. He was arrested in April 1943 for his outspoken opposition to Hitler and executed by hanging in a concentration camp in the last days of the war on 9 April 1945. His book *The Cost of Discipleship* has become a modern classic.

- **Blessed Oscar Romero** (1917–80) – in many respects a traditional bishop of the Church (Archbishop of San Salvador) until he underwent a conversion following the death of his good friend Fr Grande at the hands of El Salvador's death squads in 1977. He became a prophetic voice in his country, speaking out against poverty, state brutality and injustice and was killed by a single bullet as he said Mass on 24 March 1980.

- **Pope Francis** (b. 1936) – could be used as an exemplar of many Gospel values, but speaking out against corruption in the Mafia and the Vatican Curia, among others, makes him an outstanding example of a modern prophetic voice.

Gospel Value no. 5 – Simplicity
non-attachment to wealth

At the beginning of his first encyclical, *Evangelii Gaudium* ("The Joy of the Gospel"), Pope Francis took many by surprise when he identified the greatest problem we face today: not sexual decadence, not relativism, not even violence, but consumerism, or "the desolation and anguish born of a complacent yet covetous heart, the feverish pursuit of pleasures, and a blunted conscience. Whenever our life becomes caught up in its own interests and concerns, there is no longer any room for others, no place for the poor."[11] Pope Francis, who took his name from the poor Saint Francis of Assisi, was very much in tune with his Lord when he wrote those words. Jesus does not show any interest in acquiring material possessions or status and consistently sides with those who have neither. Luke is the strongest of the Gospel writers in insisting that wealth is an obstacle to discipleship. People who are worried about their wealth have "choked" (8:14) the word of God inside them.

In Matthew's Beatitudes, the poor "in spirit" (Matthew 5:3) are blessed. Matthew's community seemed to contain more wealthy people than Luke's. Joseph of Arimathaea is mentioned in all four Gospels, but only in Matthew is he described as a "rich man… who was also a disciple" (Matthew 27:57). Luke seems to be serving a poorer community. In his parables he writes about small amounts of money, such as the widow's "two small copper coins" (21:2). In his Beatitudes it is the "poor" who are blessed. He does not spiritualise them as

Matthew does. Does this mean that Jesus is blessing poverty? No, the poor in Luke's Gospel are the *ptochoi*, those who are impoverished and marginalised, literally crouched and beggarly. This is not a state to be desired. Luke Timothy Johnson comments that when Jesus says that the kingdom of God is theirs, it "does not imply rule within the realm, but acceptance by God within the restored people".[12] Jesus is not saying that in his kingdom their poverty will be reversed – although he does encourage his disciples to stand against injustice; rather, he is saying that these loveless ones are loved by his heavenly Father.

The disciples of Jesus have always experienced a tension between the expectations of their calling and the expectations of the culture in which they live. Today that tension is especially acute. There are many who call themselves Catholic who have exactly the same aspirations as most of the culture around them towards material wealth and comfort. The conversation at so many of the social gatherings I have attended over the years has been about house prices, promotion at work, salary, perks, bonuses, windfalls, *when we win the lottery*! Thankfully, we have prophetic voices to shake us out of this dream, like Jean Vanier, the founder of L'Arche, the communities across the world for adults with learning difficulties. He writes about the "tyranny of normality"[13] which blunts our conscience and seduces us into the mindset of the prevailing culture. He believes that the solution lies in what he calls the "sacrament of encounter". Faith, he says, "is not the preaching of an ideal life, but above all a meeting with one person: Jesus".[14] And where do we encounter Jesus most directly? In the poor, the injured, the last, the lost and the least. "The meeting with the person who is poor, humiliated and rejected can transform us and show us the deep meaning of our life."[15]

Key Quotations from Luke

"Therefore I tell you, do not worry about your life, what you will eat, or about your body, what you will wear." (12:22) – Do Not Worry

"You cannot serve God and wealth" (16:13) – The Parable of the Dishonest Manager

"How hard it is for those who have wealth to enter the kingdom of God!" (18:24) – The Rich Ruler

Gospel Values in Action

• In what ways can your school provide an "encounter" with those who are poor – allowing our students to grow in understanding of the different types of poverty and deprivation?

• Are we vigilant about the messages we provide for our students about the material culture in which we live and what they should aspire to? Do we actively promote the caring professions and charities as a vocational pathway?

• Do we invite our students to "live simply so that others might simply live" (CAFOD) and grow in understanding about how the world's resources might be better looked after and shared?

Exemplars of Gospel Values: Simplicity

• **Saint Francis of Assisi** (1181–1226) – Francis was born into a wealthy mercantile family and enjoyed the high life until his slow conversion led him to a life of complete poverty and simplicity. Francis was known for his love of nature as well as the poor, and he founded the Franciscan order.

• **CAFOD** – the Catholic Agency for Overseas Development – was born when volunteer members of the National Board of Catholic Women organised the first Family Fast Day on Friday, 11 March 1960. Two years later CAFOD was officially registered and since then has inspired and supported Catholic schools and the wider Church in its mission to alleviate poverty. (http://cafod.org.uk)

• **Shane Claiborne** (b. 1975) – a Christian activist and author, a leading member of the New Monasticism movement and a founding member of the "intentional community" called the Simple Way, in Philadelphia, Pennsylvania. He advocates a Gospel lifestyle of simplicity, non-violence and service to the poor. He is the author of *The Irresistible Revolution: living as an ordinary radical*.

Gospel Value no. 6 – Humility
lack of ego, dependence on God

One of the many original aspects of the teaching of Jesus was the attention he paid to children. In the ancient world, the young were not generally considered to be an object of admiration. Geza Vermes, the Jewish scholar and historian of early Christianity, says that "the elderly wise man is the biblical ideal".[16] When people brought "even infants" (Luke 18:15) to Jesus, they were rebuked by the disciples. This behaviour was clearly against a cultural norm. But Jesus wants to see the children and not just to use them as a visual aid. His revolution of tenderness extends to every man, woman and child. No one is beyond his blessing. The point he does make with the children in front of him is that to be receptive to the kingdom you need to be like a child: trusting, powerless, open, pure in heart. You can't bring your own agendas to the kingdom. There is only one reference point, God the Father. What is required is complete trust in his will.

In another example of how the early disciples didn't always get all the messages, Paul clearly considered the behaviour of a child inferior to that of an adult: "When I was a child, I spoke like a child, I thought like a child… when I became an adult, I put an end to childish ways" (1 Corinthians 13:11). Vermes considers the stress Jesus places on a childlike attitude to God an "astonishing novelty"[17] which was not readily adopted by his disciples. They were often found to be engaged in some kind of power struggle, arguing over who was Number One. In fact, at the moment of greatest crisis, on the night he was betrayed and was offering them

his body and blood in a final act of remembrance, a row breaks out "as to which of them was to be regarded as the greatest" (Luke 22:24). We've been arguing about status ever since, but Jesus is adamant that it should not be like this. He uses the image of the child again to make his point: "the greatest among you must become like the youngest, and the leader like one who serves" (22:26). It's reassuring for today's Christian leaders to know that it takes a while for this message to become interiorised, even when you've lived with Jesus. Some of them struggled with the remarkable proclamation from Jesus that "I am among you as one who serves" (22:27). What other lord or leader had ever spoken like that?

The importance of humility before God is also illustrated in the parable of the Pharisee and the tax collector. The introduction is unusually explicit and directs the readers to the target of the parable, which is those who trusted in themselves and "regarded others with contempt" (Luke 18:9). The Pharisee and the tax collector both go to the temple to pray, but the gulf between them in the eyes of the people is thrown into reverse in God's perception. As we've noted previously, the Pharisees were not held in general contempt, but tax collectors were. Luke Timothy Johnson comments that the Pharisee's prayer "is all convoluted comparisons and contrast; he can receive no gift because he cannot stop counting his possessions. His prayer is one of peripheral vision."[18] The tax collector's, in poignant contrast, is "utter simplicity and truth".[19] The only thing he brings to his prayer is his own inadequacy, and "because he both needs and recognises his need for the gift he receives it".[20]

Key Quotations from Luke

"God, be merciful to me, a sinner!" (18:13) – The Parable of the Pharisee and the Tax Collector

"Truly I tell you, whoever does not receive the kingdom of God as a little child will never enter it." (18:17) – Jesus Blesses Little Children

"The greatest among you must become like the youngest, and the leader like one who serves" (22:26) – The Dispute about Greatness

Gospel Values in Action

* Does your school have any discourse about servant leadership at all levels?

* What are the signs and symbols of leadership in the school? Do they reflect a Gospel understanding of leadership as service?

* Is humility explicitly extolled in the school and arrogance understood to be undesirable?

Exemplars of Gospel Values: Humility

* **Mary, Mother of God** – devotion to Mary the Mother of God has fallen away in many Catholic schools and in the Church generally. We need a new devotion to Mary, without some of the excesses of sentimentality we have seen in the past. Mary does not feature a great deal in the Gospels, but salvation history would not have been the same without this young Jewish girl's remarkably humble response to God's invitation to bear a son: "Let it be with me according to your word" (Luke 1:38).

* **Saint Thérèse of Lisieux** (1873–97) – Thérèse died when she was just twenty-four, having lived as a cloistered Carmelite nun for less than ten years. Thérèse, like Mary, has gone out of fashion for some Catholics who have dismissed her as an example of sentimentalised piety, but this saint is worthy of rediscovery, and her "little way" of trusting in Jesus and coping with the daily demands of life in community has much to teach us.

* **Blessed Charles de Foucauld** (1858–1916) – like many holy men and women in the history of the Church, Charles started off as something of a dissolute character before undergoing conversion at the age of twenty-eight. He was drawn back to the faith during an expedition to Morocco when he saw how devout Muslims were. He was inspired by the "life of Nazareth", the humble and hidden years Jesus spent in a small village in Galilee before his public ministry. He entered contemplative life before going to live with the Tuareg tribespeople in the Sahara, where he was killed by bandits in 1916. Like Francis of Assisi, he wanted to "shout the Gospel with his life".

Gospel Value no. 7 – Preferential option for the lost and the least

As noted in the previous chapter, the context for Luke's three "lost and found" parables at the beginning of Chapter 15 was the contrast between the tax collectors and sinners, who were drawn to Jesus, and the Pharisees and scribes, who were grumbling about Jesus' table fellowship with the lost, those who had placed themselves beyond the law by their way of life. The first story he tells by way of response is the parable of the lost sheep. Unlike the parables of the lost coin and the lost son, which are both unique to Luke, the story of the lost sheep also features in Matthew's Gospel. But even this short parable is treated differently by the Gospel writers. Matthew's context is instruction to the disciples on greatness and the importance of the little ones, while in Luke the parable is actually addressed to those who are lost and those who should treat them better. In Matthew, the shepherd goes after the one lost sheep out of a hundred, and "if he finds it" (Matthew 18:13) he rejoices. In Luke the shepherd seems much more determined and goes after the lost sheep "until he finds it" (15:4). Only in Luke do we find the tender detail of the shepherd laying the sheep on his shoulders, and only in Luke are friends and neighbours called for a party to celebrate the return of the lost one.

Leaving the ninety-nine to seek out the one stray was a strategy which may have made sense to shepherds who didn't want to lose any of their sheep, but the modern mind resists such a calculation: why not concentrate on the ninety-nine who want to be here rather than waste resources on the one who doesn't? Caiaphas, the high priest, certainly came to that conclusion when he reasoned that "it is better for you to have one man die for the people than to have the whole nation destroyed" (John 11:50). One person is dispensable for the greater good. Today's corporate world might also think that way, but any institution which claims to follow Jesus is called to think in a different way. The logic of God is not the world's logic and we must struggle with that in school when we have one child whose egregious behaviour is causing a disturbance. I have been in that position as a head teacher more than once and reasoned that it would be better for the community if he or she was removed. Jesus doesn't provide advice to school leaders on exclusion policy, but he does, in Luke's Gospel, describe a God who looks for the lost until they are found, which challenges us to do our utmost, and then some more, to find and bring home our lost sheep.

The same point is made when Luke describes a direct encounter between Jesus and Zacchaeus. As a "chief tax collector" (19:2) and by implication one who amassed wealth from the people by corrupt practice, Zacchaeus was beyond the ministry of the Pharisees and held in contempt by the people. But somewhere in his heart there is a stirring towards Jesus when he comes to town. With the crowds pressing in as always, Zacchaeus needs to climb a tree for a better look, since he is short in stature. What happens next is worth paying attention to. Zacchaeus doesn't say anything – it is Jesus who looks up and says, "Zacchaeus, hurry and come down; for I must stay at your house today" (19:5). It's the same pattern we saw before: welcome, table fellowship and *then* conversion, which in the case of Zacchaeus, unlike the law-abiding rich ruler we saw in the previous chapter, involves giving to the poor and making generous reparation for his fraudulent activity. It's not just the Pharisees who don't like this approach: "all who saw it began to grumble" (19:7). The exclusive attitude of the Pharisees was not confined to their group; it had popular support. But that was never a concern for Jesus. In what could be his mission statement, he tells the grumblers that "the Son of Man came to seek out and save the lost" (19:10).

Key Quotations from Luke

"But when you give a banquet invite the poor, the crippled, the lame, and the blind." (14:13) – Humility and Hospitality

"Rejoice with me, for I have found my sheep that was lost." (15:6) – The Parable of the Lost Sheep

"The Son of man came to seek out and save the lost." (19:10) – Jesus and Zacchaeus

Gospel Values in Action

- What is the attitude of the school to students who are "lost" in terms of their behaviour or in any other ways which put them outside of the "mainstream" of school life?

- Does your school permanently exclude students as a very last resort or are exclusions used to "make a point" about what good behaviour looks like?

- Do the students routinely hear the message in assemblies and lessons that the "lost" of society have dignity in the eyes of God?

Exemplars of Gospel Values: the preferential option for the lost and the least

- **Saint John Baptiste de La Salle** (1651–1719) – another saint of the Church who came from a wealthy background but was converted by his encounter with the poor. He was ordained a priest in 1678 but gave up his family home to devote himself to the education of the poor, moving in with teachers and forming the community that would be known as the Brothers of the Christian Schools. De La Salle was known for his innovative educational methods and was made the patron of teachers in 1950. http://www.lasalle.org

- **Saint Vincent de Paul Society** – an international Christian voluntary organisation dedicated to tackling poverty and disadvantage by providing practical assistance to those in need – irrespective of ideology, faith, ethnicity, age or gender. The Society is a lay organisation initially formed in Paris in 1833 by Blessed Frédéric Ozanam and his companions, and has been active in England and Wales since 1844. Placed under the Patronage of St Vincent de Paul, it is inspired by his thinking and works. SVP groups can be found in many Catholic schools, with Mini Vinnies for the younger students and Youth SVP and B-Attitude for the older ones. http://svp.org.uk

- **Jean Vanier** (b. 1928) – a modern prophet, wonderful spiritual writer and founder of L'Arche (http://www.larche.org.uk) and Faith and Light (http://www.faithandlight.org.uk) worldwide networks of support and sanctuary for adults with learning difficulties. You can find out more about his life and work at http://www.jean-vanier.org.

Gospel Value no. 8 – Love
generosity, magnanimity

The word "love" appears in Luke's Gospel, as we have seen above, in the Sermon on the Plain. There must have been a ripple through the crowd the first time Jesus said, "Love your enemies" (6:27). For the God-fearing people of Israel this was a step beyond what the law required of them. Luke Timothy Johnson tells us that "Luke prefers to think of this characteristic Christian attitude in terms of a verb… It means to will the good of another."[21] Luke makes this clear himself in the next phrase when Jesus says, "Do good to those who hate you" (6:27). There is no danger of this point being lost in the interpretations of a parable. This is the unambiguous revelation of the divine nature: universally loving.

The loving nature of God in Jesus is expressed not just in words but in the other major dimension of his ministry: healing. The charismatic renewal movement in the Church has brought back the language and practice of healing which was largely lost for many years. The modern mind seemed more content to focus on the verbal expressions of the ministry of Jesus and we explained away the miracles, subjected them to rational scrutiny or dismissed them as legendary. James Martin SJ provides a robust response to this attitude. He tackles the assumption that miracles were common in stories about powerful figures in antiquity, a kind of convention almost. He refers to the work of the German scholar Gerhard Lohfink, who says that stories about major personalities who performed miracles were "extremely rare in antiquity and well attested miracles were even more uncommon".[22] He concludes that "Jesus is depicted as definitely a miracle worker, and a great many miracles are attributed to him, something that is unique in antiquity".[23]

Raymond E. Brown supports this thesis with reference to non-Christian sources, especially the Jewish historian Josephus, writing in the AD 90s, who described Jesus as "a doer of wonderful deeds".[24] This is not a pious reaction to the modernist tendency to dismiss the miraculous, but the view of informed scholarship. And why wouldn't Jesus perform healing miracles? It is entirely consistent with an understanding of a loving God who willed the good of others, especially those in "bondage" (Luke 13:16) to sickness. In most cases it is the faith of the person which allows them to be cured: "Daughter your faith has made you well; go in peace" (Luke 8:48). In Mark and Matthew's Gospels there is a suggestion that Jesus' miraculous powers were more limited when he encountered "lack of faith" (Matthew 13:58).

In the previous chapter we considered the love of God manifested in Jesus' gift of his body "given" (22:19) for us from the moment of the incarnation and still available to us now in risen form in the Eucharist and the scriptures. We have seen Luke's emphasis on the lavish generosity of God in the response of the father to the prodigal's return. It is the "best" (15:22) robe which is draped around the son's shoulders and the "fatted calf" (15:23) that is prepared for the banquet, not a goat. If we are open to this flow of grace, if we give, then "it will be given" (6:38) to us, and not in a miserly fashion, but "a good measure, pressed down, shaken together, running over, will be put into your lap" (6:38). God is not pusillanimous, small-spirited, counting up our trespasses in some divine ledger. No, he is magnanimous, big-souled, recklessly generous. Paul might not have got the point Jesus was making about being a child but he really got the point about the centrality of love (see "Reflections from Scripture" at the end of this chapter).

Key Quotations from Luke

"Love your enemies, do good to those who hate you." (6:27) – Love for Enemies

"Even the hairs of your head are all counted." (12:7) – Exhortation to Fearless Confession

"This is my body, which is given for you." (22:19) – The Institution of the Lord's Supper

Gospel Values in Action

- Are the miracles of Jesus presented to your students as the "deeds of power" of a loving God who wills our good?

- Does your school have a "loving culture"? What aspects of the life and practice of the school make it more or less loving?

- Does your school hold generosity and magnanimity in esteem, including generosity with time?

Exemplars of Gospel Values: Love

- **Saint Peter** (martyred c. AD 65) – the career of the first pope is a fascinating journey from doubt, confusion and denial to love unto death. St Peter should be a great comfort to those disciples who get it wrong a lot and feel themselves weaken. In the Acts of the Apostles he can't not proclaim the Good News of God's revelation. He is smitten.

- **Saint Maximilian Kolbe** (1894–1941) – Raymund Kolbe (Maximilian was his religious name) was inspired by a vision he had of the Virgin Mary when he was twelve. He became a Conventual Franciscan Friar and during the war he stayed in his monastery and helped thousands of Jewish refugees. He published anti-Nazi pamphlets and was arrested and sent to Auschwitz. He volunteered to take the place of one of the men who had been sentenced to death by starvation as a warning not to attempt escape.

- **The Trappist monks of Tibhirine, Algeria** – in 1996 a group of Trappist monks living peacefully with their Muslim neighbours in Algeria were kidnapped and killed by fundamentalists. The 2010 film *Of Gods and Men* tells the story of the events leading up to their death, including their decision to stay with the community they loved rather than return to the safety of France.

Gospel Value no. 9 – Forgiveness
reconciliation

The miracles of Jesus are in some cases preceded by forgiveness, making the point that healing of the soul and reconciliation to God are more important than physical healing. This is illustrated in the healing of the paralysed man in Luke's Gospel. It is another wonderfully vivid story. Jesus was preaching indoors, perhaps in a courtyard area shared by a number of houses. The crowd is packed in so there is no way the paralysed man carried on a bed by his friends can get anywhere near Jesus. But they are determined and somehow get him up onto the flat roof and make a hole to lower him down. What a commotion that must have been. They do not say anything to Jesus, but when he sees "their faith" (5:20) he forgives the man. It is only when he is challenged by the Pharisees about this that he heals the man physically to show that "the Son of Man has authority on earth to forgive sins" (5:24).

The Gospels describe the incomprehension the disciples felt at times with the forgiveness of God. In Luke, Jesus says to his disciples that "if the same person sins against you seven times a day, and turns back to you seven times and says, 'I repent' you must forgive" (17:4). Luke lacks the hyperbole in Matthew's account when the disciples are told to forgive "seventy-seven times" (Matthew 18:22), but as Luke Timothy Johnson points out, "the phrase 'a day' stresses the quotidian character of discipleship".[25] For Luke, discipleship is a daily experience for which the "daily bread" (11:3) of God's word is necessary sustenance. It is in the daily reality of life in our schools and colleges that our commitment to forgiveness and reconciliation will be tested.

When a young person commits a misdemeanour, how do we respond, what do we "see" in front of us? A problem, a naughty child, forever labelled as "trouble"? In Luke's Gospel, a woman who had been forgiven by Jesus of her sins, "which were many" (7:47), gatecrashes the house party of a Pharisee to smother the feet of Jesus with grateful tears. Her burden has been lifted, the emotional levee breaks. Jesus exposes the Pharisee's position with the gently ironic question, "Do you see this woman?" (7:44). The point is that he does not see a woman at all but a ritually unclean thing which should not be touched. Jesus sees one who has been forgiven, "hence she has shown great love" (7:47). In other words, that is why she shows great love; she is not on her knees begging for forgiveness. Jesus never humiliates the sinner; only the rule-bound human authorities do that.

As a head teacher I am acutely aware of the daily challenge of the message of forgiveness and reconciliation in our schools. There may come a point when the safety of the community demands that one student must leave, but only after we have done our utmost to achieve reconciliation. There have been striking developments in secular thinking on restorative justice which should be employed in our schools as a means of reconciliation. When there is a rupture in relations between students or between staff and students, our values insist that we work towards reconciliation. This is skilled and patient work and requires a commitment to the training of staff. There are also many striking examples in our society of forgiveness and reconciliation, some but not all inspired by faith. Many of these stories, including the work of the family of Jimmy Mizen which will be familiar to many Catholic schools, are gathered together on the website of The Forgiveness Project (http://theforgivenessproject.com). For a Christian community these are exemplars of how we are called to respond to hurt, by the grace of God.

Key Quotations from Luke

"Be merciful, just as your Father is merciful." (6:36) – Love for Enemies

"Father, forgive them, for they do not know what they are doing." (23:34) – The Crucifixion of Jesus

"Peace be with you." (24:36) – Jesus Appears to His Disciples

Gospel Values in Action

• Does your school practise restorative justice when relationships are broken?

• Does your school make it clear to students who have been in the wrong that they are forgiven and not forever labelled as a troublemaker?

• Is the sacrament of reconciliation offered to the students in a way which helps them to understand the mercy of God? Is an equivalent found for students who are not Catholic?

Exemplars of Gospel Values: Forgiveness

• **Saint Stephen** (martyred c. AD 34) – Stephen was the first Christian martyr and died the way Jesus died. He was filled with the Spirit, spoke out bravely in front of the people, did not resist his captors and forgave them as they stoned him to death. The execution was approved of by Saul, who would later undergo dramatic conversion to Christ (Acts 7:54–60, 8:1).

• **Family of Jimmy Mizen** – following the murder of sixteen-year-old Jimmy Mizen in a bakery in Lewisham in south-east London, the Mizen family and local community have been determined that something good will come from it. For more information on the work for peace and reconciliation of the Mizen Foundation visit http://forjimmy.org.

• **Corrymeela Community** – the Corrymeela Community was founded in Northern Ireland in 1965 by the Reverend Dr Ray Davey, whose experiences in World War II as a prisoner of war and a witness to the Dresden bombing made a profound impression on him. He founded Corrymeela as a centre for reconciliation in society. For more information on the inspirational work of this community down to the present time visit http://www.corrymeela.org/.

Gospel Value no. 10 – Hope
resilience, perseverance

Apart from love, the other two virtues which will "abide" (1 Corinthians 13:13) in Paul's great hymn to love are hope and faith. Only Luke and Matthew have infancy narratives, and it is there we find the first signs of hope in the Gospels. The angel Gabriel tells Mary that she will conceive and bear a son who "will be called the Son of the Most High" (Luke 1:32). This is the hope of Israel for a Messiah coming to pass. After Jesus is born, his parents present him in the temple as required by the law, and there they meet Simeon, a pious Jew who was "looking forward to the consolation of Israel" (Luke 2:25). We are meant to understand that Jesus fulfils this role, which is why Simeon can now go in peace, for his eyes have seen the salvation of God. Jesus is not only the hope of Israel but the hope of the world, as Luke has already made clear by placing the infancy narrative in the context of world events. It is not mighty Caesar, but the humble Jesus who is the saviour of the world.

In his public ministry Jesus brings hope to the hopeless, but he doesn't mean the hope of liberation from the Romans, he means liberation from the violence and absurdity of the human condition and not knowing how to be reconciled to God. In Luke's Beatitudes, the third one is "Blessed are you who weep now, for you will laugh" (6:21). This is the "good news to the poor" (4:18) which Jesus proclaimed as a defining feature of his mission in the synagogue at Nazareth. Whereas Matthew's Beatitudes speak of internal dispositions ("poor in spirit" [Matthew 5:3]) which will produce certain

results, Luke Timothy Johnson points out that "Luke describes objective conditions that will be or are being reversed by God".[26] This is fundamental to the Christian view of reality: there is hope, there is meaning to life, there is consolation for those who weep. This hope should permeate any Christian community, especially a community of young people. Our schools should be places of hope and joy.

At the end of Luke's Gospel the risen Lord appears to two disciples walking on the road to Emmaus on the Sunday after the traumatic events of Good Friday. Interestingly, they had heard reports of an empty tomb, but that is not enough to prevent them leaving Jerusalem in a state of utter despondency. Not knowing it is Jesus they're speaking to, they tell the stranger that they "had hoped" (24:21) that Jesus was the one to redeem Israel. They are a type for many people today, for all the lost and disillusioned of every generation. They had placed their hope in a prophet and he came to his end as prophets always do: consumed by the system, a threat removed, order restored. They extend hospitality to the stranger and it is only when he leaves them that they are granted the realisation that this was Jesus. They remember how their hearts burned within them on the road as he explained the scriptures to them, how they recognised him at the breaking of the bread.

Their hope is ignited again and "that same hour" (24:33) they go back to Jerusalem and find a community reeling with the visions of the risen Lord. He appears to them again with his message of reconciliation and tells them to go out and proclaim "repentance and forgiveness" (24:47) to all nations. When the Lord leaves them for the final time at

Bethany they "returned to Jerusalem with great joy" (24:52), knowing that their hope was secure. What we are seeing at the end of this Gospel is a scattered community coming back together, and in Luke's next book, the Acts of the Apostles, we will see this community receive the Spirit of God and grow in faith and the confidence to go out and tell the world the Good News of the risen Lord Jesus Christ. As our trusted guide Luke Timothy Johnson says, "Faith in Jesus as Lord was based on a continuing, transforming experience of transcendent power in communities, and not simply on experiences that people had on Easter day."[27]

Key Quotations from Luke

"Blessed are you who weep now, for you will laugh." (6:21) – Blessings and Woes

"The Lord turned and looked at Peter." (22:61) – Peter denies Jesus

"And they worshipped him, and returned to Jerusalem with great joy." (24:52) – The Ascension of Jesus

Gospel Values in Action

• Do you promote the character traits of resilience and perseverance in the Christian context of hope?

• Is there a spirit of joy in your school? Bad days notwithstanding, is there a deep sense of hope and therefore joy in the daily reality of the school? If not, what might be the obstacles to this?

• Are we open to the educational philosophies which support resilience and perseverance, such as the theory of Mindset?

Exemplars of Gospel Values: Hope

• **Saint Paul** (martyred c. AD 65) – in his second letter to the Corinthians, Paul reminds his listeners of what he has suffered for the sake of the Gospel: floggings, beatings with rods, stoning, shipwreck, bandits, hunger, thirst, sleeplessness, cold (2 Corinthians 11:23–33). It would have finished off most of us, but that *metanoia* he experienced on the road to Damascus seemed to propel him around the known world on fire with the Gospel of Christ, no matter what the personal cost.

• **Viktor E. Frankl** (1905–97) – Frankl's account of surviving in Auschwitz and his struggle to find hope in the most brutal experience of the human condition was published in *Man's Search for Meaning* and is an inspiration.

• **Nelson Mandela** (1918–2013) – the South African anti-apartheid leader who served as President of South Africa from 1994 to 1999 was the country's first black president and the first elected in a fully representative democratic election. Mandela served twenty-seven years in prison on charges of conspiracy to overthrow the State. When he became president he emphasised reconciliation between racial groups and established the Truth and Reconciliation Commission. He was awarded the Nobel Peace Prize in 1993.

Reflections by Catholic Leaders in Education

The Catholic head teachers I interviewed were generally comfortable with the discourse of Gospel values. However, some tension was exposed between a focus on the Gospel and the totality of the Catholic faith; in other words, if you just focus on the Gospels then you're in danger of diminishing the tradition, the teaching of the Church developed over hundreds of years, arising from the Gospels and inspired by the Holy Spirit. I will come back to this point in the next chapter. It was also striking that while most leaders were more comfortable with the discourse of values and could provide examples of values in action, it was not always clear that Gospel values were an embedded part of the school's understanding of its mission.

❧

As I've said in my own research, having interviewed quite a large number of Catholic head teachers, they slot Gospel values into their discourse but they never specify what this means, so it is unfortunately used as a shorthand slogan, but we've certainly got to be articulating and, more importantly, we've got to be practising Gospel values, but we've got to specify what are these Gospel values. So I've suggested that from the reading of the Gospel, there are many values you can derive and obviously faith, hope and love are obvious priorities and then I've tried to specify others that seem to me to be absolutely Gospel values that our schools should be embodying:

reconciliation, compassion, community in solidarity, respect for all people of all talents, celebrations and breaking bread together. The students should experience those in their schooling life and then they've a concrete encounter with what Gospel values are.

—Professor Gerald Grace, Director of the Centre for Research and Development in Catholic Education, St Mary's, Twickenham

Our learners sometimes look quite aggressive and might have a few choice words that they can throw at you, despite their social disability, and they don't always come across as friendly, nice people and when we go into a social context in public people will look alarmed, disdainful, they will tut and they will frown because they're not following the norms of nice behaviour. But what we find here is that really quickly you see through that shell on the outside of aggression and unpleasant behaviour and you see that core; you see that really frightened lovely person inside and that's who you communicate with all the time, not the monster bit on the outside, but that core. And you're trying to get that core to come out and be the whole person. I think that pretty much every one of our staff members here communicates with and loves that inner God, the Christ child inside every single one of them, and that's what they're connecting with.

—Annie Sutton, Executive Principal, St Joseph's Special School, Cranleigh

We had the Mizen family visit the school in January as part of our Year of Mercy to talk about what happened to their son, Jimmy, and the forgiveness that they've shown. That definitely inspired our young people and I had a girl in the prep school who wrote to the Prime Minister about it and asked what the government was doing to stop crime and protect young people in the country. In fairness, the Secretary of State did write back, which was lovely, but to do things like that would give children and young people examples of people really living out Gospel values.

—Sarah Conrad, Head of Prep School, St Teresa's, Effingham

It does warn you about being persecuted within the Beatitudes – when we stand up for what is right then people speak all kinds of calumny against you, and I think our children live in an age where they can't get away from the opinions of other people. They follow them by text, they follow them through Facebook, they follow them through the whole of the media world and other people's opinions have become proportionally more important to young people. What we need to do therefore is, when we're thinking about how we put the Gospel values into action, we need to make sure that we're focusing on the skills that enable them to be able to stand up and be true to themselves and not worry about other people's opinions or what they read about themselves on Facebook and Twitter and things like that.

—Diocesan Officer, Catholic Diocesan Education Department

I think the Acts of the Apostles are really useful for giving you ideas of how values/virtues can

be applied and how they cannot be applied, how it doesn't work out. You can see these disciples coming to terms with the death and resurrection and they're thinking, well, we're going to live like that, but then when you get to apply it in real life it doesn't always work out like that. You get those tensions, you might bring St Paul's letters in here, you can see the real tensions. Trying to think, well we've got a vision for community – how do we apply it? How do we get it to work and have those Christian values in our community? And I think reading through there, you can get some idea of the struggles that those early Christians have, trying to put values/virtues into practice and I think that's really important to remember when we're talking about values in schools because it is a struggle. It's not like, we can choose these values and if everybody applies them it'll all be wonderful. There are tensions between the values, tensions between forgiveness and justice sometimes. Certainly when I talk to children it's a struggle sometimes with forgiving everybody and having justice, proper justice.

—Dr Ann Casson, Research Fellow at National Institute for Christian Education Research (NICER), Canterbury Christ Church University

"Gospel values" is a term that I've not been terribly happy with because to me it sounds as if you're taking Catholicism and you're trying to make it a bit more acceptable, so it sounds like a phrase that's been conjured up not to scare people, if you like, because everybody agrees that in the Gospels there are some wonderful values shown, but in a sense to reduce Catholicism, which is a very complex and broad thing and a very well-worked-out thing, obviously rooted in the Gospels, but to reduce it just to a focus on values that we can extract from the Gospels seems to me rather limiting and while obviously I think we should have a focus on the Gospels and what they teach us as a school, it should be more than that. So we don't tend to use the term "Gospel values" and never have done and I haven't changed that because I do feel it's a bit limiting for a Catholic school.

—Stephen Oliver, Principal, Our Lady's Abingdon

Reflections from Scripture

If I speak in the tongues of mortals and of angels, but do not have love, I am a noisy gong or a clanging symbol. And if I have prophetic powers, and understand all mysteries and all knowledge, and if I have all faith, so as to remove mountains, but do not have love, I am nothing. If I give away all my possessions, and if I hand over my body so that I may boast, but do not have love, I gain nothing. Love is patient; love is kind; love is not envious or boastful or arrogant or rude. It does not insist on its own way; it is not irritable or resentful; it does not rejoice in wrongdoing, but rejoices in the truth. It bears all things, believes all things, hopes all things, endures all things. Love never ends. But as for prophecies, they will come to an end; as for tongues, they will cease; as for knowledge, it will come to an end. For we know only in part, and we prophesy only in part; but when

the complete comes, the partial will come to an end. When I was a child, I spoke like a child, I thought like a child, I reasoned like a child; when I became an adult, I put an end to childish ways. For now we see in a mirror, dimly, but then we will see face to face. Now I know only in part; then I will know fully, even as I have been fully known. And now faith, hope and love abide, these three; and the greatest of these is love. (1 Corinthians 13:1–13)

But I say to you that listen, Love your enemies, do good to those who hate you, bless those who curse you, pray for those who abuse you. If anyone strikes you on the cheek, offer the other also; and from anyone who takes away your coat do not withhold even your shirt. Give to everyone who begs from you; and if anyone takes away your goods, do not ask for them again. Do to others as you would have them do to you. If you love those who love you, what credit is that to you? For even sinners love those who love them. If you do good to those who do good to you, what credit is that to you? For even sinners do the same. If you lend to those from whom you hope to receive, what credit is that to you? Even sinners lend to sinners, to receive as much again. But love your enemies, do good, and lend, expecting nothing in return. Your reward will be great, and you will be children of the Most High; for he is kind to the ungrateful and the wicked. Be merciful, just as your father is merciful. (Luke 6:27–36)

CHAPTER 4

Eight Signs of a Gospel-inspired School

– CHAPTER 4 –

Eight Signs of a Gospel-inspired School

The list of values drawn from the Gospel in the previous chapter is in no way "canonical" or official. There have been attempts by the diocesan education services of other countries to set out a framework for Gospel values (see, for example, *Values for Life* published by the Scottish Education Service), and each one comes up with a slightly different list. We have already mentioned the Gospel values outlined by Marcus Stock in *Christ at the Centre*, based exclusively on the Beatitudes of Matthew. Fr Adrian Porter, in his comments in Chapter 1, reflects on the work of Jesuit schools in drawing up a Pupil Profile, or eight pairs of virtues which pupils in Jesuit schools can aspire to. There is of course a great deal of commonality in all of this work. The Church documents, inspired by the Gospel, have a number of core themes running through them, as you would expect. In this chapter we will try and identify those themes, or characteristics, that make Catholic schools distinctive. Or to put it another way: what does a school look like that is inspired by the Gospel? What would be its defining characteristics? I have chosen eight, based on a reading of Luke's Gospel, the Church documents, the reflections of leaders in Catholic education and my own experience as a Catholic head teacher.

1. Inspired by a Supernatural Vision

A government spin doctor a few years ago is reported to have said, "We do not do God." I have often used that line at open evenings for prospective parents to make the point that Catholic schools do not agree with that: *we do God*. We need to start there because the very notion of the transcendent is becoming a fading memory in our society. The divine is being written out of the script. If the Catholic school is inspired by the Gospel, then it is inspired by a Lord whose identity was shaped in relation to the divine, his Father in heaven. As we saw in Chapter 2, Jesus was inspired for his mission by the love of the Father which was revealed to him in many ways, including mystical prayer experiences, like the Transfiguration (Luke 9:28–36). Jesus revealed this God to us and the good news is that he is compassionate and forgiving and he loves us with a reckless abandon. This is what gives human beings a profound dignity and what gives Catholic schools their anthropology, their understanding of the human person.

Gaudium et Spes, Vatican II's Pastoral Constitution on the Church in the Modern World, began with an affirmation of the inherent dignity of the human being, "the noble calling of humanity and the existence within it of a divine seed".[1] This is foundational for Catholic schools and provides the rationale for all our policies and practices, our day-to-day behaviour. Everything from safeguarding to health and safety on school trips is inspired by this fundamental insight of our faith that as human beings we have a divine origin and an eternal destiny. The document goes on to say that this belief in the inherent dignity of every human being demands that we respect difference and oppose discrimination in any shape or form, since "every type of discrimination affecting the fundamental rights of the person, whether social or cultural, on grounds of sex, race, colour, class, language or religion, should be overcome and done away with, as contrary to the purpose of God".[2] This is not the same list as the "protected characteristics" outlined in the Equality Act of 2010, but neither, I think, is it meant to be exhaustive, since it says *every* type of discrimination is contrary to God's purpose.

So we inhabit a different world, a different universe, to the mainstream. We see young people as spiritual beings invited into a relationship with a loving God. We resist any vision of education which promotes knowledge acquisition *solely* for the sake of material success or advancement. Archbishop Miller, formerly Secretary to the Congregation for Catholic Education, puts it strongly when he says: "If Catholic educators, parents, and others who dedicate themselves to this apostolate fail to keep in mind a high supernatural vision, all their talk about Catholic schools will be no more than a 'gong booming or a cymbal clashing' (1 Cor 13:1)."[3] And this supernatural

vision determines our perception not only of the person but also of the world. Dermot A. Lane describes the world according to the vision of Vatican II as a "graced reality, a sacred place and a holy space where we can find God if we look hard enough".[4] Our schools are invited to promote a theologically rich educational vision which sees the world as enchanted and grace-filled, original sin notwithstanding, and which sees human beings as inherently dignified and worthy. Our schools are invited to find and protect sacred space and sacred time so that our young people can experience the divine life within them and "discern in the voice of the universe the Creator whom it reveals".[5]

2. Jesus Christ is the Foundation

God is revealed to us in Jesus Christ and "Christ is the foundation of the whole educational enterprise in a Catholic school".[6] There is a school of academic thought which considers Church documents on education to be filled with vague and abstract phrases. This statement, which I have always considered to be key, is reported by Sean Whittle in his research as an example of "Catholic edu-babble",[7] one of many unhelpful slogans throughout Church documents on education. When I was visiting Catholic schools for my research into *How to Survive in Leadership in a Catholic School* I met one primary head teacher who told me that every Monday morning at assembly he read the Sunday Gospel because he knew that most of the children would not have heard it the day before. If the Gospel is what the children hear first thing in the morning and if Gospel values are the inspiration for the decisions adults make in the community, then no, that statement is far from edu-babble, it makes perfect sense in the real world of Catholic schools.

It is also a statement that identifies an urgent need. The most recent document from the Congregation for Catholic Education, *Educating Today and Tomorrow: a renewing passion*, came to the conclusion that "Catholic schools are often the only places where young people encounter the bearers of Good News".[8] This is a significant admission from the Church. It is a recognition of what we have known for some time, that most of the young people in our schools do not go to church and do not hear much about the faith at home; and more and more of them in fact are not from any kind of Christian background. In the wider culture, as noted already, God and religion have largely been written out of the script. The language, norms and assumptions of a religious view have all but disappeared in a digital age of "widespread superficiality",[9] where image and information are preferred to depth and reflective wisdom.

Simply by sharing the Gospel with our young people, in age-appropriate and engaging ways at assemblies, class prayer and liturgies, we are fulfilling our central purpose, which is to provide "an encounter with the living Christ".[10] We have to lead them there in ways which we might not have anticipated a decade ago. In recent years, the first thing I've had to do with the new intake of Year 7 students was to teach them the sign of the cross and organise a "teaching Mass" for them. I have seen the numbers of students willing to go to confession after a service of reconciliation decline sharply. The assumptions of the Catholic culture which many in my generation took for granted no longer apply. So what are we to do? Persevere against the tide to make good Catholics out of our students, when many are not baptised? Persevere with those who are Catholics and risk marginalising those who are not? Or bring them to the essence of the Catholic faith, which is the charismatic and counter-cultural figure of Jesus Christ?

Young people warm to this driven character who railed against hypocrisy and adult casuistry, sided consistently with "the lost" and tried to show his friends what love meant. He talked all the time about a "reign of God" which reversed the age-old values of power, prestige and possessions. He called people to change their mindsets, *to change the direction in which they looked for happiness*. He challenged our definition of what it means to be a human being. This should inspire us to ask the same question: what does it mean to be a human being, to be fully alive, in the light of this revelation? As the Church has always said, Christ is the Teacher. We are tempted by other agendas and success criteria (those distortions of the kingdom), but the Church keeps prompting us to remember what we are about, remember the values of Jesus Christ.

Archbishop Miller says that "Catholic schools have the task of being the living and provocative memory of Christ. All too many schools fall into the trap of a secular academic success culture… Christ is 'fitted in' rather than being the school's vital principle."[11] Professor Gerald Grace takes up the same theme in his comments at the end of this chapter. As a head teacher I have often succumbed to these temptations and given the impression to staff that the only things that matter are the "headline" outcomes and our Ofsted grade. With the pressures of accountability and parental expectations to get young people into university, it is no surprise that many of my colleagues experience the same temptation. However, as we will explore later on, a commitment to excellent outcomes for young people is not incompatible with the mission of a Catholic school. It is making these outcomes our sole purpose, our "treasure", that compromises our purpose.

3. A Spirituality of Communion

In the Acts of the Apostles, Luke's sequel to his Gospel, he describes how those first Christians, "devoted themselves to the apostles' teaching and fellowship, to the breaking of bread and the prayers" (Acts 2:42). The "fellowship" among Christian groups, or *koinonia*, has always been central to their self-understanding. The most painful moment in the life of the community, which we have seen too often in the second millennium of Christianity, is when the *koinonia* is broken and one group sets out on its own, or is expelled. The Catholic school, which is a community of the Church, should value and promote this deep fellowship, based on the anthropology we described above. If we live in community *as if* every member of that community has an intrinsic dignity, if we live in community *as if* the values of Jesus Christ inspired how the community functioned, then the school should be distinguished by a "special atmosphere animated by the Gospel spirit of freedom and charity".[12]

Catholic schools, as I have said, are communities of the Catholic Church. They proceed *"ex corde Ecclesiae*, from the very heart of the Church".[13] We invite our young people to encounter Jesus Christ in the rites and traditions and lived reality of the Church. The community experienced in our schools should be an encounter with the wider community of the Catholic Church, past and present, the communion of saints. One of the questions which leaders can ask themselves is what experience of the community of the Catholic Church do our pupils have at school? Especially for those with no knowledge of the Church, it should be positive and life-affirming. It should be an invitation to join in the life of the Church, the prayers and liturgies, since we believe that is fundamental to being human. Clare Hogg, in her reflections, provides an excellent example of students, Catholic and non-Catholic alike, enjoying the liturgical life of the Church while on a trip to Lourdes. Ann Casson reflects on the importance of prayer and worship in the school, and how we prioritise such "non-measurable" but fundamental aspects of our identity. In fact, if there is one thing that distinguishes our schools in this day and age, it is that we *pray*.

Students and their families should know what they are signing up to when they enter a Catholic school. I always made it clear to parents that in our school we say prayers, we have Mass, and the students who are not Catholic are invited to come up for a blessing at communion. In my experience the students, Catholic or not, have always responded well to Mass, even if it's only a chance to take "time out" and reflect on life for a while. One of my best memories was when we organised a Mission Week and invited in youth teams and Spiritan priests from England and Africa. Our final Mass was a true experience of the global community of the Church, with the Gospel acclamation sung beautifully in Swahili and Fr Patrick dancing in procession with the Gospel held over his head as if it was the one great treasure in his life. I couldn't have told you that day which students were Catholic and which were not and it wouldn't have mattered to me. For many students it was the highlight of their year.

Our school communities should furthermore be places characterised by a warm welcome and warm relations between staff and students. Friendly, but not familiar. In my research, when I asked students to describe to me what their Catholic school was all about, they often used the phrase "family atmosphere". This is as it should be. The students should feel safe and happy and very much "at home". And what about the staff? How can we balance the needs of "performance" with this atmosphere we have described? Again, if we follow through our commitment to Catholic anthropology then we have a duty to develop the staff and foster "appreciation of the various charisms and vocations that build up a genuine school community".[14] Governors employ adults for various roles in the school, but seeing staff develop and grow far beyond those original roles in a spirit of support and encouragement is one of the real satisfactions of headship. What happens when they don't fulfil those roles, we'll consider in the next chapter.

Of course, there are times when the community gets tired and tetchy. What school community in the dark days of November or the cold days of January is not

tested in its patience? Saint Pope John Paul II, in *Novo Millennio Inuente* ("At the Beginning of the New Millennium"), provided us with a memorable description of a spirituality of communion. This spirituality is based on the "mystery of the Trinity dwelling in us, and whose light we must also be able to see shining in the face of the brothers and sisters around us".[15] This light is not always easy to see on those cold fractious days but that does not change the reality. It does, however, encourage us to "know how to 'make room' for our brothers and sisters, bearing 'each other's burdens' (Gal 6:2) and resisting selfish temptations which constantly beset us and provoke competition, careerism, distrust and jealousy."[16] Like the Gospel itself, it is a counter-cultural message and seems almost impossibly idealistic, but that is the kind of community we are called to bring into being.

The world in which we live and for which we are preparing our young people does at times pay homage to community and teamwork, but more often than not the lived experience of our culture is one of individualism and self-interest. The Catholic school, in as much as it lives out a spirituality of communion, will show our young people another way which, in the words of the 2002 document from the Congregation for Catholic Education, *Consecrated Persons and Their Mission in Schools*, promotes the "overcoming of individualistic self-promotion, solidarity instead of competition, assisting the weak instead of marginalization, responsible participation instead of indifference".[17] The document also encourages leaders to ensure that Catholic schools are run as "places of encounter, listening, communication, where students experience values in an essential way".[18] They should never, as Annie Sutton says in her reflections at the end of this chapter, be a dictatorship. That is the way of Caesar, not Jesus.

4. A Curriculum of the Head, Heart and Hands

So when a school community inspired by Gospel values, with a spirituality of communion informing its behaviours and relationships (albeit imperfectly), gets down to lessons on a Monday morning, what does that look like? Until the advent of the academy programme, all state schools in England and Wales were required to teach the National Curriculum. Academies and independent schools do not have to teach the National Curriculum but their programmes of study will still be determined "backwards" by the public exams they are preparing their students for and the curriculum content will end up looking broadly similar to that of maintained schools. So where does the Gospel fit into all this? The 1977 document *The Catholic School* produced a definition of the educational purpose of Catholic schools as follows:

> Its task is fundamentally a synthesis of culture and faith, and a synthesis of faith and life: the first is reached by integrating all the different aspects of human knowledge through the subjects taught, in the light of the Gospel; the second is growth of the virtues characteristic of the Christian.[19]

Sean Whittle sees this as another example of

Catholic edu-babble,[20] and although it's not a phrase I would use, in this case I think he has a point. The concept of integrating all aspects of the curriculum in the light of the Gospel does not stand up too well to the glare of academic inquiry. It is a concept which needs development, since the document itself does not provide an answer, nor is there much specific guidance anywhere else in Church documentation. It also begs a number of further questions about the purpose of the curriculum in a Catholic school. Do our schools exist to educate Catholics, as was the case in my Catholic schooling, or to provide a Catholic approach to education?

The 1988 document from the Congregation for Catholic Education entitled *The Religious Dimension of Education* provides a useful distinction between "catechesis", or personal growth in the faith, which "happens most especially in a local Church community",[21] and the aim of the school, which is knowledge, and specifically Religious Education which "tries to convey a sense of the nature of Christianity and how Christians are trying to live their lives".[22] Other documents widen the aim of the school beyond knowledge, but I think in this instance this particular definition was used as an antithesis to catechesis, rather than being intended as a full definition of the aim of the school. It seems to me a prescient statement about the reality of Catholic schools today which I have alluded to above. Many of our students are not Catholic, or are nominally Catholic, and do not want to be catechised, or "re-catechised". Since more and more of our staff are not Catholic and there has been a steady decline in the percentage of staff holding the Catholic Certificate in Religious Studies (CCRS), neither would we have the resources for such an approach.[23] What is needed now, and what is possible, is an education, or a presentation of reality, which is rooted in the Gospel. Then we might be able to make sense of a curriculum "in the light of the Gospel".

If the Gospel values we outlined in Chapter 3 are broadly understood and accepted by the community (and the challenge there lies in staff training, but it is more achievable than training staff to be catechists), this provides a "lens" through which to view the curriculum content. It is an approach which is actually not far from what the government expects from schools, which is a curriculum that promotes the spiritual, moral, social and cultural development of pupils. This is our version of that duty, our foundational perspective through which to view topics in the curriculum. Ann Casson, in her reflections at the end of this chapter, provides an excellent example of how Gospel values feature in the normal educational discourse of one school. At the end of each lesson, the students and teacher together reflect on the Gospel values they have covered in the course of the lesson. The school is not trying to make good Catholics, but it is trying to educate young people in a Gospel perspective.

Trevor Cooling, in *Doing God in Education* (2010), provides many examples of how theological themes can be introduced into subjects in the curriculum. I heard Professor Cooling speak at a head teachers' conference sometime around 2010 and I was struck by his suggestion of using the parables in language lessons, instead of the usual unimaginative litany of everyday items. Again, the ultimate demands of public exams might hamper that approach, but I felt it

was well worth exploring. Today, many commentators call any attempt to introduce faith into the curriculum indoctrination, but we must be prepared to argue that no education is value-free. The so-called liberal or Enlightenment approach to education is premised on a view of reality. It may try and insist that knowledge must be based on empirical evidence, but that is a particular point of view and one that Catholic educators would argue does not do justice to the depth, richness and mystery of the human condition. It is the subject of another book to plot Gospel values fully against the curriculum – or the work of an interesting INSET day, perhaps.

The Catholic Church, if not always clear about what an integrated curriculum should look like, has at least always argued for a rounded education, for the "formation of the human person".[24] This is more than just the acquisition of knowledge – it is the ambition to develop harmoniously "the physical, moral and intellectual endowments"[25] of students. This is an argument for what is called the co- or extra-curricular dimension of our schools. I know some schools where this has been downplayed for the sake of a better focus on exam results, but that is not a Catholic vision of education. In the final statement of the World Congress for Educating Today and Tomorrow: A Renewing Passion in 2015, Pope Francis argued for the benefits of an "informal education" since "formal education has been impoverished due to the legacy of positivism".[26]

This positivism only conceives of what Pope Francis calls the "language of the head" and what the *instrumentum laboris* referred to as a "merely functional view of education".[27] Pope Francis urged educators to open new horizons, not to be afraid to offer the rich tradition of Christian art and music, to develop sport and physical activity. He said there are three languages: the head, the heart and the hands, and the Catholic school should speak all three. Of course our students need to think, and to think well (and we'll look in the section below at why that is important), but they must also understand and speak the language of the heart, developing emotional literacy in a world which is increasingly emotionally intemperate and incoherent; and the language of the hands, an active life which takes risks and encounters the wider natural environment, develops team work and problem-solving, all the more important as our young people are tempted to spend their days in virtual environments which require minimal physical engagement or human contact.

5. A Preferential Option for the Lost and the Least

The next sign of a school inspired by the Gospel should on the face of it be straightforward. Jesus in his public ministry consistently showed a particular affection for the marginalised of society: the lost, the least and the last. In his radical expansion of the Law he made it clear that the kingdom of God was about more than loving God and your neighbour, it was about loving God in your neighbour, especially your downtrodden neighbour. In Luke's Gospel, as we have seen, the poor have a special influence with God and the rich are constantly challenged to give away possessions if they wish to embark on the path of Jesus. *Gravissimum Educationis* ensures that this Gospel priority is written into the Church's

understanding of the mission of its schools:

> This Sacred Council of the Church earnestly entreats pastors and all the faithful to spare no sacrifice in helping Catholic schools fulfil their function in a continually more perfect way, and especially in caring for the needs of those who are poor in the goods of this world or who are deprived of the assistance and affection of a family or who are strangers to the gift of faith.[28]

It is worth noting those three categories of young people the document identifies as the priority for Catholic schools. First of all, the poor in the goods of this world, the indigent, the "poor" in Luke's Gospel (6:20). Some Catholic schools will have higher numbers of children from socially deprived backgrounds than others. Independent schools, maintained schools and academies in affluent areas or with demanding criteria for admissions may not have many children that would fall into the category of "poor" (although we will look in a moment at other forms of poverty). Whether the Catholic school has one or one hundred children who fall into this category, the Church insists that they are cared for as a priority. In state schools there has been some convergence with the government's agenda in the form of the Pupil Premium. Catholic state schools will have their Pupil Premium Action Plans like everybody else, but those of us teaching in such schools are called upon to look hard at the time and human resource we *actually* devote to children from deprived backgrounds. Our mission must also extend to their families, often but not always fractured, and we must look at how we "reach" them and involve them in an education system which many feel has let them down. Catholic schools are well known for their outstanding pastoral care, but we must continually evaluate that provision to ensure it is effectively focused on the areas of greatest need.

The second category in the document consists of those who are deprived of the assistance and affection of a family, or what we would now call Looked After Children. As we saw in Chapter 1, these children have some of the highest figures for mental health issues and the lowest outcomes in educational performance. Again, the State also insists that these most vulnerable children are considered first when any decisions are being made about support and resources. In my experience, Looked After Children often have other layers of need, such as special educational needs or medical needs. I have also found over the years that a disconnect can easily open up between management aspirations for these children and their daily reality: do all teachers in the school know who the Looked After Children are? Is that taken into account in seating plans, lesson plans, homework strategy (for those who do not have a home environment conducive to homework), the marking of books, intervention and support? Is the Looked After Child particularly gifted? Have we explored any "hidden" gifts and allowed them to flourish? We shouldn't have to wait for Ofsted to tell us that these children are a priority. The Church told us that fifty years ago.

The third category takes us back to the earlier points about the purpose of Catholic education: is it for baptised Catholics, or is it for others as well? *Gravissimum Educationis* is somewhat confusing in

this regard. It says that the purpose of the school is to "help youth grow according to the new creatures they were made through baptism".[29] In the next paragraph, the statement we have been examining then states that the third category for priority are those "who are strangers to the gift of faith".[30] Sean Whittle suggests that this reflects the tensions around the drafting of the document itself: "There had been eight draft versions of the document and up until the sixth, it had the title 'The Catholic School'. The change in title reflected a desire to formulate a more inclusive stance."[31] As noted above, subsequent documents made it clearer that the purpose of the Catholic school was not for the catechesis of Catholic children but rather to offer children an education according to the vision of the Catholic Church. In most Catholic schools, baptised Catholics still have priority in admissions, but there are many strangers to the gift of faith in our schools and we provide an invaluable service to the Church by being for them a face of Christ.

The Catholic School on the Threshold of the Third Millennium, published in 1997, recognised "new forms of poverty"[32] in the developed world. While Catholic schools still served the needs of the physically poor, there was a new mission to "those who have lost all sense of meaning in life and lack any type of inspiring ideal, those to whom no values are proposed".[33] That could be a description of many of the young people today in our more affluent society. They have smartphones and branded clothes, but they sometimes "come from families which are broken and incapable of love".[34] I have known these young people and meeting their needs can be a challenge, but that is what the Church calls us to do:

"to these new poor the Catholic Church turns in a spirit of love".[35] *Educating Today and Tomorrow* further extended our understanding of the poor in our schools: "Those who find themselves in greater difficulties, who are poorer, more fragile or needy, should not be seen as a burden or obstacle, but as the most important students, who should be at the centre of schools' attentions and concerns."[36] The definition is widened again to include any who are vulnerable. The best practice I have seen is when a school keeps a Register of Vulnerable Students and carefully monitors the level and impact of support offered to each student, with an identified key worker to lead the intervention.

The Church has often referred to a preferential option for the poor, but there is a mission to everybody, no matter what their material circumstances are. As we've noted already, some maintained schools, academies and independent schools may educate students from more affluent areas or backgrounds (although any student from any background can fall into the category of "fragile and needy"). Some independent schools, though by no means all, educate students from wealthy backgrounds. The Church documentation on education does not distinguish between state and independent schools. They are both Catholic schools, part of the same Catholic Church, with a mission to bring the Gospel, the Good News, to young people (and their parents). Matthew's Gospel was written with rich people in mind – rich people who were also disciples. When people of wealth are converted to the Gospel, they have an important role in supporting the mission and can play an influential role in public life.

6. Social Justice and Transformation

Another aspect of the mission of the Catholic school which has been consistently clear is a commitment to the common good of society. I remember in my Catholic upbringing there was a good deal of suspicion about "social action", which was regarded as being too political, a bit too communist. Looking back, I think that was a result of the Church's concerns during the Cold War about the spread of Godless ideologies. Beginning again with *Gravissimum Educationis*, the purpose of the Church and its educational function is described as "the perfection of the human person, the good of earthly society and the building of a world that is more human".[37] This is inspired by the teaching and action of Jesus, who was not passive in the face of oppression and injustice. It is true that in order to navigate through the opposition he faced he had to be circumspect at times and used parables to make his point, but he was clearly offering more than a private "salvation plan" to get to heaven. He referred to a kingdom or reign of God throughout his ministry which involved a liberation for the poor and downtrodden. He did not advocate violence to achieve this kingdom but, rather, a reign of love and compassion. If people actually loved their neighbour and their enemies, then society would look quite different.

We do not invite the young people in our schools to look at the world in a neutral way. We say that homelessness in our society is unacceptable, that the treatment of workers in sweatshops is unjust, that the treatment of women and girls in many societies is demeaning, that the despoliation of the planet for our luxury items is violence against our common home – *because it is contrary to the Gospel*. We do not and cannot compel our students to take action, but we can say that the view of the Church is that we should act and invite them to do likewise: "since it is motivated by the Christian ideal, the Catholic school is particularly sensitive to the call from every part of the world for a more just society, and it tries to make its own contribution to it".[38] This takes us back to the commitment to standards of education in our school. If a central part of our mission is to educate boys and girls to contribute to making the world better, then they will need knowledge, skills and qualities not only to understand how things work for the advantage of some and the disadvantage of others, but to know how things can be changed. High levels of literacy, numeracy and all the other skills the curriculum offers are not only necessary for the dignified growth of the individual, they are needed for effective social action. Academic excellence, then, becomes a means of social transformation: "knowledge is not to be considered as a means of material prosperity and success, but as a call to serve and to be responsible for others."[39]

The pedagogy of the Catholic school, likewise, should serve this end. *Educating Today and Tomorrow* comes out firmly against rote learning and a functional or solely economic view of education. It argues for a range of skills to be developed to help our students to become active and principled citizens – "skills related to consciousness, critical thinking and creative and transforming action".[40] Critical thinking was not a notable feature of my Catholic upbringing. You basically learned the truth about salvation, this world and the next, and that was that. There was nothing to discuss. That view has changed considerably and the Church now recognises the need for young people to be critical and evaluative. There is no explicit consideration given to what happens when young people turn these critical faculties on the Church, but we should be prepared for that. We cannot close down debate. Our schools should be forming curious, compassionate, canny minds a bit like the mind we saw in action in the Gospels: a perceptive, caring, emotional intelligence that can see through hypocrisy and lies, knows the right questions to ask and is brave enough to challenge the vested interests.

There are many agencies in the Catholic Church that support such an approach. For years the Catholic Agency for Overseas Development has been producing resources to support Christian social action. Many schools now have their own CAFOD Action Group or something similar. Young people will generally respond well to calls to support the vulnerable or distressed in charitable action, but we have been called to more than just a few enjoyable "mufti" days. We have been called to run schools which educate young people in the skills, knowledge and motivation necessary to transform the world. The American professor of theology and religious education Thomas H. Groome said: "If we could come to see our students not as people to be made into 'good Catholics' or 'good Baptists' or the like, in a narrow sense, but rather as people who are called upon to engage in the world for the making present of the kingdom of God … then imagine what the transforming consequences might be for ourselves, our church, our society, and our world."[41]

7. A Culture of Vocation

Catholic schools are distinctive, according to Bishop Marcus Stock in *Christ at the Centre*, when they, among other things, "engender a culture of vocation".[42] The phrase leads to a footnote with a reference to the publication we mentioned in Chapter 1, *New Vocations for a New Europe*, sometimes known by its Latin title, *In Verbo Tuo*, the final document of the Congress on Vocations to the Priesthood and to Consecrated Life in Europe (Rome, 5–10 May 1997). That tantalising clue is worth following up on since the document is a rich resource which deserves much wider attention, or "unpacking", in Catholic education. For those of my generation who were brought up with the notion of vocation as a calling to the priesthood and religious life, it provides a much deeper definition, and one which our young people need to hear about. Everybody has a vocation by the very nature of their existence:

> The vocation is the providential thought of the Creator for each creature, it is his idea-plan, like a dream found in God's heart… Every creature expresses and is called to express a particular aspect of the thought of God. There he finds his name and identity.[43]

We have a duty to promote careers in schools, at least from Year 8 onwards in maintained schools, and this is important work. We need to help our students understand what skills and talents they can bring to a jobs market which requires much greater flexibility to survive and thrive than it did twenty years ago. Most young people will have done a number of jobs before they are thirty, if indeed they can find jobs, so that aspect of our work in schools is crucial. What is being offered in *In Verbo Tuo* is a theological understanding of each individual as called by God according to his divine plan. Jesus demonstrated this in his ministry by calling people out of sin and indifference to new life. His encounters were "an opportunity for confronting the person with the strategic question: 'What will I do with my life?', 'What is my path?'"[44] We see him again and again setting people on the way to life – "Your faith has saved you; go in peace" (Luke 7:50). The role for teachers and school leaders is spelled out with great emphasis: "True vocations promotion can be carried out only by those who are *convinced* that in every person, no-one excluded, there is an original gift of God which waits to be discovered."[45] This is not dissimilar to the point we started with about the intrinsic worth of each individual.

There is a National Vocations Framework (see http://www.ukvocation.org/) which provides many helpful resources. There is no programme for schools as such, but there is enough material to inspire Catholic leaders. In my time as head teacher we developed a few simple initiatives which helped to engender a culture of vocations. One Lent, we asked our students the question Pope Benedict asked young people during his apostolic visit to the United Kingdom in 2010: "What kind of person do you really want to be?"[46] We introduced this idea with an assembly to prepare the ground and provided some prompts: this was not a careers inventory or an excuse to be silly, so no *Star Wars* references please! It was a genuine invitation to our students to reflect on their lives and how they would like to mature. After the assembly the tutors led smaller group discussions, prayerful reflection times with readings, then over a period of a couple of weeks invited all the students to write their final answer on pre-printed postcards. At our school Mass at the end of Lent students from each tutor group brought up their cards at the offertory procession. We then made displays (anonymised) around the school, which I noticed the students were drawn to.

What was striking and actually very moving was how positive these cards were. We collected in almost 800 in total, and overwhelmingly the students wrote honest, heartfelt and positive messages about wanting to make a difference. They were not just writing what they thought their tutors wanted to hear since they had the option to write anonymously. We did have some silly comments, but that was very much a minority. Many of the comments left an impression on me, like the Year 8 boy who said, "I want to be the better version of me", or the Year 9 girl who said she wanted "to forgive those who were the hardest to forgive". What we did achieve was to engage all the students in thinking about vocation in a deeper way than *what I want to do when I grow up*.

Another idea which worked was having a Vocations Day during our Mission Week with a specific focus on vocations to the priesthood and religious life. We were joined on the day by several priests and nuns who spoke in very down-to-earth terms at year group assemblies and then visited classes to take questions from the students. At the very least the students got to speak to real men and women who had given their lives to follow the path of the Gospel. In my youth we had four or five priests in each parish and nuns teaching in the schools. These people were part of

our day-to-day experience. Today, one overworked priest looks after four or five parishes. There just isn't the same connection and the void is often filled by negative stories in the press. We should continue to hold out to our young people the possibility of a calling to the priesthood or religious life.

Finally, we asked each of our faculties (my experience is in secondary schools) to think of one inspiring life they would hold up to the students as an example of a calling to serve. We had some interesting discussions about whether or not they had to be Catholics or saints, but I decided to open up the role to anybody who had contributed to the good in the world. We had some "good Catholic" choices like Mother Teresa and Pope Francis, but we also had Alan Turing from the maths faculty, which prompted a number of points for discussion, especially among the older students, of issues ranging from the morality of wartime intelligence to the treatment of gay people in this country up until the 1950s. Again, these examples of lives given over to some great work inspired discussion throughout the school about vocation and what you might do with your one precious life. In my day it would have been all about the lives of the saints, and as I've said in Chapter 3, the saints remain inspiring figures for us, but as Vatican II told us, "humanity is being continually stirred by the Spirit of God",[47] and it is good for our students to encounter examples of that.

8. Gospel-inspired Leadership

All of the above can only happen if there is Gospel-inspired leadership in the school. There are many good people in our schools who are committed to this agenda, but it tends to weaken if it is not led and encouraged by senior leadership. There is still some doubt and confusion among Catholic leaders about the extent to which the Catholic head teacher is a faith leader. I have heard head teachers resist this description, or react with embarrassment when it is applied to them. I have heard some clergy speak in opposition to such a description as if it in some way threatens their role. The very fact that there is doubt shows perhaps that we do not have a strongly embedded common language to describe Catholic headship, and that would be welcome. In fact, it will be necessary in the years ahead. With the continued push towards academy chains in the state sector, more and more of our most skilled leaders will find themselves running multi-academy trusts and will be labelled "chief executives" by the system. They will fulfil this role well, of course, but they should be helped not to lose sight of their deeper role as faith leaders.

Catholic education is an apostolate of the Church and head teachers are lay ministers in that apostolate. It is matter of concern that there is no *national induction programme* sponsored by the Church for men and women who take up this key role. Each diocese will do its own thing, some better than others, but there is no common curriculum, if you like, for what the Catholic head teacher needs to know, and no common understanding of how they can grow in this role. That is a significant piece of work and it requires a concerted effort from all the dioceses if we are to continue to develop leaders in the Catholic sector. In the next chapter I will simply try and outline some of the "signs" or characteristics

of a Catholic leader who is driven and inspired, not by success criteria or the desire for power, status and prestige, but by the Gospel.

Reflections by Leaders in Catholic Education

The phrase "Gospel-inspired school" was new to most of the Catholic leaders, but nevertheless they were able to speak with confidence out of their own experience about what characterises or distinguishes their schools as Catholic Christian. This is the lived experience of our leaders. For this question there was a strong sense of convergence and consensus around what makes a school distinctively Catholic, especially the priority given to the poor and vulnerable, the formation of the whole person, the sense of service and commitment to the common good, the positive and supportive atmosphere in the school, the opportunities to take part in a wider curriculum and in the wider life of the Church. Over several research projects, I have noticed that while there may be variations in the language used (and some uncertainty about what constitutes Gospel values), there is a remarkable degree of unanimity about the purpose of Catholic schools and what they should look like in practice. I have encountered very little confusion in our schools as to what we are about.

ନ

I think we have got to be able to show that we don't only talk about values, that we apply them in given situations of challenge. The application of market forces into schooling at the moment does encourage schools to develop a sort of culture of being an individual successful market leader and we have to see in that a great temptation because our commitment, if we are applying our Gospel values, is always to show commitment to the common good and therefore wherever possible we should seek to have partnership relations among other schools to do almost the Good Samaritan thing and to be helping a school that is in serious problems. When I say that, "successful" schools, I put successful in quotes because the secular world's judgement of a successful school would be very different from our judgement of a successful school. Theirs is very much about measurement and product in its outlook. Ours is much more holistic and inclusive of what we mean by successful schools. Support relationships among schools with the successful and wealthy and those in nice areas to be stretching out to those in deprived areas, it shouldn't be that the government should be forcing schools to do that. It ought to be the living out of Gospel values in practice.

I tried to sum it up there by saying the signs of the Gospel-inspired school will be when most of its teachers do not act only as professionals but also as professionals and witnesses, using the famous statement of Pope Paul VI, "Modern man listens less seriously to teachers than he does to witnesses and if he does listen to teachers it's because they are also witnesses." [48] That is one of the most profound but brilliant statements ever made. That would be the sign of a Gospel-inspired school, that most of the

teachers act as professionals and witnesses and then, added to that, most of its students do not act only as achievers (I'm an achiever, look at me). Yes, we want achievers, but in the service of the common good. If such a school exists, those are some of the signs of the Gospel alive in that school.

—Gerald Grace, Director of the Centre for Research and Development in Catholic Education, St Mary's, Twickenham

The next point of contact is for those who, in the case of St Mary's it would be the majority, wouldn't be coming from within a Catholic tradition, either staff or students, how do you bring people along with you? So people may not share and they may not know the values, they may not share directly the confession that supports the values but they may like the attributes, they may want to be here. So people will talk, when you talk to staff or students, people talk about community, they talk about friendliness, they talk about the commitment to the way that we run the university and the operations – that we pay the London Living Wage, we mostly don't outsource key functions like security, catering, cleaning, so we don't elevate the financial criteria above all else. We like to build and foster community. We try to put a premium on things that perhaps in other places wouldn't get the same premium because actually we want to run it along quite strong ethical lines.

So you're creating entry points that people may say, "Well I like all these things", but then you bring them to the deeper level, and that is, "Why do you think these attributes emerge?

What foundations do you think that we commit to this?" And then you begin to have the conversation around the distinctiveness, around the identity, around the values, and again how you live the values or how you try to live the values, and that can be a conversation. If the conversation isn't taking place it's worrying. The fact that it is taking place with some people saying we need to do more to embed these values and other people basically saying, I'm confused by these values. And that is when you are into a work in progress, it's a lifetime's work, it's about communication, it's about explanation, it's about witness.

—Francis Campbell, Vice-Chancellor, St Mary's University, Twickenham

When the Jesuit General came to Britain a couple of years ago he gave us a challenge, he said make sure that in your institutions you're asking what can we do at the margins, somewhere else completely. So, the kind of example you might use is, all of our schools have a partner school in the Third World or the developing world somewhere, at least one, if not two or three. But equally we've done some big projects on homelessness in our schools, which, especially in London, is a huge problem and so we have these homelessness sleep-outs, we do a lot of development work around that and it seems to me that what you're doing is you're not going to change the homelessness situation but in a school-appropriate way we're educating young people to understand why people are homeless, what

they can do, etc. And I think that where you have a school that's kind of smug and content and doesn't really see itself as relating to anything, there's a problem, but you can bring things into the classroom in a safe, controlled way that's educational.

—Adrian Porter SJ, Delegate for Education for the British Province of the Society of Jesus

I think the single thing that struck me most was the mission to the poor and the preferential options for the poor and really challenging myself about what that means. It's one thing when it was perhaps a religious order working in an inner-city environment and they were providing a service for children who wouldn't otherwise get education, but what does that mean in an independent school where children may not be hugely wealthy but there's not definite material poverty and then thinking about where are the other sorts of poverty – emotional poverty and I think particularly I would say spiritual poverty. How do we then reach out as a community to those who it seems have nothing in that sense, they live in a world where they make material [gain] out of everything but spiritually seem to be very poor, and how do we meet that need? There will be schools where material poverty is still very real but I think in this environment there are other sorts of poverty which we are having to meet.

—Charlotte Cummins, Senior Deputy Head, Prior Park College, Bath

The signs of a Gospel-inspired school would include visual signs such as Christian artefacts in every room with various prayers displayed. However, it must go much deeper than this. The school should be a welcoming beacon; everyone should greet each other, open doors, laughter, music, encouragement, passion for human rights and almsgiving. Every individual should be celebrated. Having just returned from a pilgrimage to Lourdes with a group of Year 11 pupils, it became evident how important this is to our pupils. The miracle of Lourdes, to me personally, is to see our young people interacting with the VIPs [the sick and infirm] and demolishing, for a short time, that most evil of poverties, the poverty of loneliness. I feel the closest to Our Lady when I see faith in action, pupils sitting and listening, tucking VIPs in to ensure they are comfortable, laughing and socialising. This is what I believe Mary meant when she asked for a Chapel to be built – the young Church taking the lead and nourishing the Church for the future.

However, listening to the testimonies of the pupils, who were both Catholic and non-Catholic, the religious ceremonies and the Masses were the highlight of their week. The realisation and encouragement that they belonged to something so much bigger than their school or parish experience both inspired and moved them. Ensuring that the worldwide Church is celebrated in school and that pupils feel part of this Church is at the forefront of my thoughts for the next academic year. The importance of knowing where the pupils are

coming from rather than presuming to understand their faith journey is essential.

—Clare Hogg, Head teacher, St Thomas More High School, Crewe

I think you should see visible signs that you are in a Catholic school. I think there should be religious artefacts around. The purpose of statues and crosses is to bring your mind back to Christ at points in the day so when you see it you think, "Yes, I mustn't forget God in my life." So I think there should be in every classroom those visible signs. Particularly in a primary classroom where you might be praying as well, that there's a prayer focus that you could turn to at those times of prayer in the day. Other signs: I think the curriculum should be a holistic one and you would like to think that, regardless of all the pressures out there with SATS and entrance exams and everything else, that we would hold to our principles and think, "This is about the whole person. We're all made in the image and likeness of God." Then in a more overtly religious way I think the curriculum should be also involving the service that we've spoken about, teaching them to be compassionate people. Giving them those opportunities to do that and helping them to develop their spiritual side through retreat programmes, reflection days, that kind of thing, so they can find who they are and think about what God's calling them to be.

—Sarah Conrad, Head of Prep School, St Teresa's, Effingham

When I was going to come here, the majority of my mainstream colleagues said don't move to special needs, it'll absolutely ruin your career. You'll never get back out. Well, I think it's true, you'll never get back out because nothing else would present the same challenge to you once you've got in, but actually I think if I did go back to mainstream now I'd be such a better teacher, such a better leader, because you get a real perspective of actually what's important and what isn't important. What's the American expression, "don't sweat the small stuff"? It made me realise that there was so much small stuff going on in secondary schools that actually you don't need to worry about, and perhaps you should just come at it on a level playing field with the young people with a lot more respect. I think we like to think that we've given them respect but actually it's like a dictatorship and that's where you get a lot of the angst and the tensions from. I'd probably be impossible to manage if I went back into mainstream.

—Annie Sutton, Executive Principal, St Joseph's Special School, Cranleigh

You have these Gospel values and you can see them coming through in worship and it may be quite easy to put values in worship. A lot of schools will have "The value of the week is…" and you can plan your worship theme around that and have quite a prayerful worship time and reflect on, how am I going to apply that value of worship in my life. But how do you get it in the everyday curriculum? In one school I'm aware of you have to get various things into your lesson plan, but one of the things you have to say was, "How am I using Gospel values in this lesson?" And the students were so used to that you could have a plenary and say, "What values have we used today?" and the teacher might have in mind one of them, "How have we used integrity this lesson?" and the children would come up with examples but they'd also come up and say actually Miss, I think we can put this one, so and so did this to me today, was kind and whatever and I'd say we used that value. And I think it's getting it to that level where the children understand the values so much that they can apply them and that they're used to it in every lesson. Not, apply ten values or sixteen values but, in this lesson we're thinking about how we could use integrity and we did it here and we did it there. You could also do the reverse: when could we have applied and we didn't?

One of the other key things I would say is worship – prayerful time for worship. In some of the best examples I've seen, that time is protected. Often worship time gets squeezed because we've got notices, we've got so much going on in schools, but if you have ten minutes, twenty minutes, every day and that's our worship time and all we're doing in that time is worship and you have prayer throughout the school. So the acceptance, the idea that the school is a place where prayer is normal, for students and teachers, I think that's really important. The other is a sense that we're a community, an actual sense of family. A lot of these schools where you feel that you belong, even if you're not that active, practising Catholic outside, but within school there's a sense of belonging to a Catholic community. So a community that's different, that is based on faith. The other key thing, I think, is the outward sign as well – "What are you doing about the outside?" It's the social action, the opportunities of social action provided within the school and the opportunities to engage with the wider community. This I see rarely but I think I would like to see them engage more with the local Catholic community, the Catholic church. The idea that we're not an island, we're within a Catholic community in our local area and in our national area, our Diocesan area.

—Dr Ann Casson, Research Fellow at National Institute for Christian Education Research (NICER), Canterbury Christ Church University

For me the moment when the chapel suddenly became very relevant was the summer holiday last year when we tragically lost a member of staff, and I was here in school during the summer holiday when one of our senior leaders had just found out and she communicated to another member of the leadership team and her first instinct was to go and sit in the chapel and I just blundered into the chapel and found her there. But her first instinct was to go into that space in that moment of shock and grief and I think that says a lot about the work that has gone on in this school to make that space sacred. But it's

an accessible sacred space. It's not somewhere you think, "We can't do that in the chapel." Because of the nature of the learners you can't have a kind of stiff approach to liturgy or worship. It's got to appeal in a sensory way to the learners.

—Dave Purcell, Head of RS, St Joseph's Special School, Cranleigh

One great value or virtue, if you like, is servant leadership at all levels. I believe servant leadership reflects the Gospel and in particular St Paul's letter to the Philippians 2:5–11 and his use of the Greek term, *ekenosen*, self-emptying. So the teacher empties himself when engaging in extracurricular activities because he's leaving the lofty heights, if you like, of the student/teacher relationship. What's that got to do with standards? This is very Salesian, from St John Bosco. If the students engage in these extracurricular activities they actually become more part of the community and it makes them more ready to engage in their academic work because they feel part of the community and that has a critical impact on educational standards.

—John Lydon, Programme Director for Catholic School Leadership, St Mary's University, Twickenham

Certainly, our vision as a school is very much to enable the children to flourish as children of God, so we take the view that they've been given talents, that those talents need to be brought out and developed through the school's ethos and that therefore we're looking at the children as a whole, so it's very much a holistic approach to their talents, whether they be academic or other talents, and so our interpretation of Gospel values is that we very much value those children as individuals and nurture them through and enable them to flourish, caring for the whole person and not seeing ourselves just as a collection of individuals but very much as a community and a family which involves the parents, the governors and various other stakeholders (if that's the right word). So we're all in this as a family together. So I would say that to me is how Catholic schools tend to be. When you go to other Catholic schools there's a lot of agreement that this is the vision of Catholic schools. I think that Catholic schools have the advantage of being able to draw on the Catholic tradition and draw on the scriptures in a living tradition that goes back 2,000 years. So you start from a very good place and you have the support of the Church, the local parish, Church documents and so on. You have a very rich background to draw on as a living community that you are part of.

—Stephen Oliver, Principal, Our Lady's Abingdon

Reflections from Scripture

Now there are varieties of gifts, but the same Spirit; and there are varieties of services, but the same Lord; and there are varieties of activities, but it is the same God who activates all of them in everyone. To each is given the manifestation of the Spirit for the common good. (1 Corinthians 12:4–7)

The day was drawing to a close, and the twelve came to him and said, "Send the crowd away, so that that they may go into the surrounding villages and countryside, to lodge and get provisions; for we are here in a deserted place." But he said to them, "You give them something to eat." They said, "We have no more than five loaves and two fish – unless we are to go and buy food for all these people." For there were about five thousand men. And he said to his disciples, "Make them sit down in groups of about fifty each". They did so and made them all sit down. And taking the five loaves and the two fish, he looked up to heaven, and blessed and broke them, and gave them to the disciples to set before the crowd. And all ate and were filled. What was left over was gathered up, twelve baskets of broken pieces. (Luke 9:12–17)

Resources for Further Reflection and Evaluation

Religious Education in Catholic Schools: a statement from the Catholic Bishops' Conference of England and Wales, May 2000, http://www.cbcew.org.uk/ CBCEW-Home/Publications/Religious-Education-in-Catholic-Schools-2000/(language)/eng-GB (accessed 29 July 2016). This statement explains the bishops' requirement that 10% of curriculum time in a Catholic school is devoted to Religious Education. It is also an important reminder to all leaders of the central importance of RE in a Catholic school.

The Distinctive Curriculum of the Catholic School: guidelines for school review (National Board of Religious Inspectors and Advisers [NBRIA], 2012), http://nbria.org.uk/downloads (accessed 29 July 2016). This document is an invaluable resource for any leadership team/governing body in the process of reviewing their curriculum and Catholic identity.

Catholic Education in England and Wales (Catholic Education Service [CES], 2014), http://www. catholiceducation.org.uk/images/ CatholicEducationEnglandandWales.pdf (accessed 29 July 2016). This is the most recent publication on Catholic schools from the Bishops of England and Wales, and it includes their five principles of Catholic education.

Sister Judith Russi SSMN, *Caritas in Action – Education and Formation in the Social Teaching of the Catholic Church* (Caritas Salford Diocese, 2015). I am conscious that throughout this book I have concentrated on Gospel values and not made reference to Catholic Social Teaching. There is of course a great deal of crossover and CST is informed by Gospel values, but I felt it would be confusing to introduce the seven themes of CST into this discussion. School leaders who wish to look further into CST are advised to begin with Sister Judith's comprehensive and engaging resource which provides learning opportunities throughout the curriculum. CST and Gospel values are interwoven and school leaders may decide how they can be implemented. One approach might be to embed CST in the curriculum (Sr Judith's model) and use Gospel values in management and public discourse in the school.

Caritas Salford Diocese, *Caritas in Action: advocacy and leadership in the social teaching of the Church*. A handbook for student Caritas Ambassadors. Ideas for actions in the school community in the UK. For further information on Caritas Salford Diocese publications, contact: Caritas in Action, 3 Ford Street, Salford M3 6DP. Tel: 0161 8172205

Pope Francis, *Laudato Si': on care for our common home* (London: Catholic Truth Society, 2015). I was aware that if I started to deal with *Laudato Si'* in this chapter under Social Justice and Transformation it would take up the whole chapter. In my last year in headship we were just beginning to plan a conference with our primary partners on how we could engage our school communities in this important encyclical by Pope Francis. This is well worth the attention of school leaders, working together across clusters of schools, or of multi-academy trusts.

CHAPTER 5

Eight Signs of Gospel-inspired Leadership

– CHAPTER 5 –

Eight Signs of Gospel-inspired Leadership

1. Spiritual Formation

The Church documents on education generally don't have a lot to say about leadership. The focus has often been on the teacher, especially the lay teacher as concern grew about the decline of religious orders in Catholic schools. The agenda has moved on again, however, and the previous assumption that most teachers in Catholic schools would be practising Catholics no longer holds. *Educating Today and Tomorrow*, published in 2014, acknowledged the critical role of the head teacher in ensuring the "living mission"[1] of the school. In order for this to happen, "a particular attention must be devoted to the formation and selection of school heads".[2] The spiritual formation of Catholic head teachers is emerging as *the* priority for the future of our schools. As many of the leaders say in their comments at the end of this chapter, a Catholic head teacher is expected to "walk the talk" – to *be* the mission that he or she articulates in public. If that is not the case, then we are open to charges from our opponents that this Catholic identity is just a veneer, with no depth or justification.

There was always an expectation that Catholic head teachers should be "practising Catholics".

A reference from the parish priest and a few questions during the job interview were normally sufficient to establish that. The 2012 revised version of *Christ at the Centre* goes into more detail about what being a practising Catholic entails. The post of Catholic head teacher, reserved for practising Catholics, requires the post-holder to "strive to model in their lives the values of the Gospel and to adhere, in the substantive life choices that they make, to the teaching of the Catholic Church".[3] Being Catholics, we assume that those substantive life choices refer to sexual choices, and some do, but there is reference later on in the document to other choices that would be contrary to Gospel values, such as dishonesty, violence and unprofessional conduct. There is also a refreshing admission that the practice of the Catholic faith "cannot be reduced to an outward legal conformity to rules or laws but it is a response of love to the God who is Love".[4]

What does this loving response mean in practice? In my experience of the Church, there has not been much attention paid to adult formation in the faith. Along with most of my generation, the assumption was that you observed the precepts of the Church and believed the teaching of the Church, and that this made you a good Catholic with a good chance of going to heaven. This wasn't enough for many people when they became adults and so they fell away from the Church. There was no real understanding of how to develop an adult faith, of what spiritual formation meant, and there wasn't much mention of the Gospel. Many of the Catholic head teachers I have met are still looking for that adult understanding of spiritual development. What does it mean to grow in the faith, to respond in love, to follow the Gospel path of Jesus? Thankfully, the Holy Spirit does not leave the people of God to struggle on their own, and there has been in recent years a remarkable springtime of prophetic voices who have developed profound and helpful insights into the adult journey of discipleship.

Richard Rohr, an American Franciscan priest, talks about discipleship in terms of transformation, of growing out of your ego-dominated false self into your true self. This is far from New Age psycho-babble. You'll find this in St Paul and other New Testament writing. The letter to the Colossians tells the believers that "you have stripped off the old self with its practices and have clothed yourself with the new self" (Colossians 3:9–10). I think we've largely ignored St Paul and not even paused to consider what he might be talking about. Rohr says that "we are charged to awaken, and much of the work of spirituality is learning how to stay out of the way of this rather natural growing and awakening. We need to unlearn a lot, it seems, to get back to that foundational life which is 'hidden in God' (Colossians 3:3)."[5] We are often invited to discover our true selves in God in what Rohr and others call the second half of life, perhaps in our forties or early fifties, just about the time we may take on a headship.

This is a calling away from ego security, tribal belonging, performance-driven satisfaction, lip service to the vulnerable and dutiful religious practice of the first half of life, and towards surrender to God in prayer, a sense of belonging to the bigger field of God's creation, humility, compassion and disinterested service of our neighbour. It is, in other words, a calling to the way of Jesus, to the "low road" to life in God. Rohr makes the point throughout his work that we are sometimes taken there by trauma, loss or suffering, an abrupt "wake-up call" that makes us reassess our priorities; or we can be taken there by a daily practice of prayerful encounter with Jesus Christ.

The two paths of encounter I have discovered in recent years and that I would recommend to Catholic leaders are lectio divina and centering prayer (the spelling reflects the American origins of this practice). Lectio divina is the ancient monastic practice of meditative reading of the scriptures. Group lectio involves the prayerful sharing of "echoes" or personal responses to a passage from scripture. In our local hub of Catholic schools we started the head teachers' meetings with lectio and the "echoes" became a sign of our growing spiritual friendship. It also drew us into deeper friendship with God, since we were getting to know him in his word. As we've said in previous chapters, we won't make much headway in our understanding of Gospel values unless we really get to know the Gospels. In the original "scheme" of lectio, there were four stages: *lectio, meditatio, oratio,* and finally *contemplatio,* which is close to what we are calling centering prayer.

Centering prayer is a modern version of the ancient monastic practice of contemplative prayer based on the more recent insight that such prayer is available to everybody, not just the mystics. Thomas Keating, an American Trappist monk, describes centering prayer as "a way of tuning into a level of reality that is always present and in which we are invited to participate".[6] The method of this prayer is simply to be silent for around twenty minutes, twice a day if possible, to give ourselves a break from the repetitive, compulsive and mostly self-obsessed activity which goes on in our heads. In that silence, which Keating calls "God's first language",[7] we consent to God's presence and action in our lives, just as Jesus did.

There is nothing especially Catholic about either of these, but I believe that practising both will bring us back with more appreciation to the sacramental life of the Church and to a richer encounter with Jesus Christ. When the sacraments become rote and ritualised then there does not seem to be any encounter and this is when many drift away. However, when we bring a renewed depth to our encounter with Christ in scripture and in prayer, then the sacramental mystery of reconciliation and the self-emptying of the Eucharist take on a more profound aspect. We will then in turn bring a new enthusiasm to the sacramental life of our school and a new depth of understanding about how to make the sacraments more relevant to our young people, especially those who are very distant from the language and practices of the Church.

What we lost to some extent in the rather juridical language of "practising Catholics" and so forth was the fact that we were all along talking about discipleship. A practising Catholic is a disciple of Jesus Christ, and the Catholic head teacher should be seen first and foremost as a disciple, or, in the thinking of Pope Francis, a missionary disciple, since the western world is very much now mission territory. The disciple is one who is called to conversion, as noted in Chapter 2, not one who is called to tick off a list of beliefs and rules. Pope Paul VI said that people gain the kingdom and salvation "through a total interior renewal which the Gospel calls metanoia; it is a radical conversion, a profound change of mind and heart".[8] I think we're only just beginning to talk that way about headship in Catholic schools, and not before time.

Gerald Grace, in his comments at the end of this chapter, links the preservation of the "mission integrity" of the Catholic school with the continual renewal of the "spiritual capital" in the school community. This is more than just knowledge of the Catholic tradition, it is an "internal spiritual strength", and the key question is where is that coming from? How is it renewed? This is not quite the language of radical conversion used by Paul VI, but it points, I think, to the same end, the need for Catholic leaders to be people of faith on a path of formation. In recent years, there have been a number of national initiatives to support the spiritual formation of Catholic head teachers, although there is much still to be done to support the spiritual formation of other members of staff.

The Catholic Head Teachers' National Retreats, which started in 2012, have grown in popularity and importance and have attracted some of the most influential Catholic writers and thinkers of our time, such as Timothy Radcliffe, Denis McBride, Christopher Jamison, Nicholas King and, from the Philippines, Sister Mary John Mananzan. Arising from that, a programme of spiritual direction for head teachers has been trialled in different parts of the country, and from 2017 a National School of Formation will begin to work with small groups of Catholic head teachers to develop their confidence and skills as advocates of transformational Catholic education. For more details of these programmes, please visit http://www.educarem.org.uk.

Catholic head teachers who have embarked on a personal journey of inner transformation should also have a healthy perspective on what they do. I know from experience that you can become consumed by the job, because it is demanding and we want to do it well, but if it takes over your life, that is not good for anyone. Life can become one dimensional (work and more work), which usually means that the small self, or false self, is in charge and the motivation for working such silly hours needs to be examined. I do not have the "answer" to the vexed question of work/life balance, since I always tended on the side of too many hours myself, but I have had a sense only recently that if you are serious about your spiritual life the very least you should do is to keep the fourth commandment and "observe the Sabbath day and keep it holy" (Deuteronomy 5:12). Jesus did not come to abolish the law, so the ancient wisdom still applies and it also happens to make a lot of sense to "not do any work" (5:14) one day in the week. And that includes emails – make it a digital-free Sabbath!

2. Connected to the Church

You will find Gospel-inspired leaders in Christian schools that are not Catholic and who will share many of the beliefs that have been discussed here. It is a cause of sadness that the body of Christ is divided into so many denominations and sub-groups. Vatican II's "Decree on Ecumenism" made it clear that "promoting the restoration of unity among all Christians is one of the chief concerns of the Second Sacred Ecumenical Synod of the Vatican".[9] So when we emphasise that we are referring to Gospel-inspired leaders of *Catholic* schools, it is not in the old triumphalist sense that we are right and everybody else is wrong, but rather in the respectful manner of the Council which recognised the Spirit of God at work in all religions – indeed, in all humanity. That said, the Gospel from the very beginning has been received by people in a community that struggled towards creedal unity.

This is fundamental to our understanding of the Catholic Church. Without any kind of agreed body of belief ("deposit of faith"), each individual would have their own version of Christianity and you'd be left with a "Jesus and me" arrangement, which of course many people today favour. The Catholic Church, as we've noted above, has in the past sometimes seemed to concentrate only on the body of belief, but nevertheless there is a need for authoritative Spirit-led teaching when it comes to faith and morals. So our Gospel-inspired head teachers are leaders of schools in a specific faith tradition which requires among other things that "religious education and religious worship will be provided in accordance with rites, practices, disciplines and liturgical norms of the

Catholic Church and any specific directives issued by the diocesan Bishop".[10] We are not starting from scratch when it comes to how we should worship or what we believe about the world. As Stephen Oliver said in his comments in the previous chapter, we are part of a 2,000-year-old tradition and there is much accumulated wisdom in that for us to draw upon. Richard Wilkin, a head teacher who has conducted his own research in this area, defines the role of the Catholic head teacher as an "interpreter, translating the beliefs and practices of the Church into a language that young people can understand and, we hope, come to love".[11]

Our head teachers, then, are connected to the universal Church and as such should make every effort to follow the Church's guidance on education. There is a lot of it and we look to our diocesan education services to produce summaries and resources, or a national induction programme to develop a common language and understanding arising out of the documents. At the very least, I would recommend head teachers and aspiring head teachers to read and study Vatican II's *Declaration on Christian Education* and the more detailed document which followed that, *The Catholic School*. It is also important to stay connected to the Church at diocesan level. When I started in headship in 2002 I had much to learn (I still do), but attending the diocesan conferences and retreats was a source of real growth for me. As the quotation from Marcus Stock's book in the previous paragraph also makes clear, the local bishop will have his own pastoral strategy and there will be much for school leaders to learn together in how that can be implemented and evaluated.

On the even more local level there is the parish or deanery with which the Catholic head teacher should form a relationship. It is perhaps easier for our primary colleagues whose school is in one parish to develop such a relationship. Our secondary schools often have large catchment areas and the local parish is one among many we may be in partnership with. Over the years we found different ways to develop our relationship with the local church, such as hosting the local deanery meetings and then inviting the priests to stay for lunch. This did fall away as more and more priests became overextended with their parish work, but there are other ways to keep in touch. What are the students doing in their local parishes? They are often coy about this in school, but a survey of their activity will be revealing and offer another way in to parish links. These experiences of the Church at local, diocesan and global level are important for the Catholic head teacher. Our Gospel is transmitted to us from within a long tradition of prayerful wisdom. We know where to go for instruction and guidance. Our schools are part of the Church and we grow within the Church, with all its imperfections, supporting each other on the journey.

3. Articulate the Mission

Catholic head teachers are the front men and women of the school, the public face, the public voice, and as such they are the ones called upon most to articulate the mission of the school – what it is all about. Foundation governors or trustees should also be expected to take on that role, but in my experience over the years it usually falls to the head. That is not necessarily the best model of leadership, but as several of the comments from leaders at the end of this chapter show, the reality is that the community looks to the head teacher as the representative of the school. What they say (or don't say) and how they say it is important. They create the weather in the school, set the tone. What they lead on and show an interest in expresses the priorities of the school. If the Catholicity is left to the RE team or chaplains, then it really is a sideshow, not the community's "treasure". When I stood up at my first open evening for prospective parents in the autumn of 2002 I thought I was just promoting my school. As the years went on, and with feedback from many parents and visitors, I realised that I was also promoting the Gospel, and that in fact you can't do one without the other. If you've just finished the presentational talk about your school and you haven't mentioned God or the Gospel, then it's not a Catholic school.

I understand the politics of local demographics and the pressure not to sound "too Catholic" for fear of scaring people away. In my most recent headship we saw the number of Catholic students fall due to the removal of the denominational transport subsidy and also because of fierce local competition. We still had to combat the perception that "you need to be Catholic to get in there!" In other words, in the eyes of the community, we were exclusive and did not have a mission for students who weren't Catholic. We didn't need to "dilute" the Catholic message or identity, but we had to work harder to help people understand that we had space for students who were not Catholic and tell them how their children might benefit from a values-driven, Gospel-inspired education. I used to joke with parents at open evenings that there was no secret plot to convert

their children to Catholicism when they weren't looking (there's still a memory in this country of "plotting Catholics"), but that instead they would be offered a different vision of reality from the mainstream atheistic and economic view. It is an attractive offer.

As well as articulating the mission to the wider community, the Catholic head teacher also has to share and develop the mission within his or her own school community. This is also a form of evangelisation, although I have never called it that in school. There is no specific time requirement of Catholic schools to review their mission, but I would suggest at least every five years for a major review. How the mission is being enacted and lived in the life of the school should of course be evaluated every year (and not just when Section 48 is pending), but a review of the mission strategy and statement is a bigger piece of work and requires careful planning (I provide more detail on how this could be done in *How to Survive in Leadership in a Catholic School*).

Again, the lead on this usually falls to the head teacher. As I mentioned in Chapter 2, I used to begin the process of mission review with the Church documents: those memorable, neat slogans about the Catholic school which some call "babble" would form the content of my PowerPoint presentation and then each group of "stakeholders" in turn would review and discuss the mission and the ways in which it could be refreshed. What it took me all those years to realise is that we should have started with the Gospel, meditating and reflecting on one Gospel to get to know the "values" first hand that were mentioned in passing in the documents. This then becomes not only an exercise in strategic review but an exercise in spiritual formation.

To be able to lead on this with integrity, the head teacher needs to have a personal relationship with the Gospel, as noted above, and a connection and commitment to the Church which interprets and promotes the Good News. This doesn't mean that the head teacher knows all the answers (see John Sullivan's comment about this later in this chapter, when he says that "nobody 'possesses' the gospel in any secure or pure way"); rather, it means that he or she is committed to a journey of growth in the faith. They need to do more than just roll out those key quotations, they need to have some interior understanding of the mission. This suggests that there is more than one possible statement about Catholic education. The foundation is permanent and secure (eternal, in fact), but as we saw from a discussion of Gospel values in the previous chapter, the words are not set in stone. There is plenty of room for emphasis, nuance and interpretation depending on the context and the individual.

My advice to aspiring Catholic head teachers when I speak to them is to ask them to write down (in no more than 500 words!) their vision for Catholic education. Having reflected on the Gospel, the documents and your own experience of the faith, what is your vision? How would you say it in your own words? When you've got some understanding of that, then you can apply it to the context of your school (and that will vary hugely across the country) and begin to fashion a public articulation of mission. We are then called upon to promote that mission in every aspect of our professional and personal lives.

We are, whether this sits comfortably with us or not, "ambassadors for Christ" (2 Corinthians 5:20), and in every setting in which we find ourselves – open evenings, staff meetings, assemblies, finance meetings, local authority conferences – called to give witness.

4. Outward-facing

Vatican II ushered in a new era of outreach for the Church. In the years following the Reformation, the Church turned in on itself and became something of a "fortress", protecting itself and its teaching from modernity and responding severely to what was contrary to God's law. In his opening speech to the Council, Pope John XXIII said that a fresh approach was needed and that the Church now "prefers the balm of mercy to the arm of severity".[12] Thomas Keating describes Vatican II as "a movement of the Spirit to make the values of the Gospel available to everyone on earth".[13] This new openness was reflected in the thinking on Catholic education. The *Declaration on Christian Education*, the document of foundation principles for Catholic education, stated that Catholic school communities should be "open to discourse with others" and do their best to "promote the common good."[14]

The Council set the agenda for Catholic schools in subsequent years: they should be committed not just to the formation of their own students but to the building of a better world. I looked in Chapter 4 at the Catholic school's commitment to social justice and transformation at home and abroad. In the educational community as well, the commitment to the common good should be applied. In today's world of shifting school partnerships and high-stakes accountability, any school can quickly find itself in a vulnerable position. Gerald Grace, in his comments at the end of the previous chapter, challenged our understanding of a school's "success" to include a sense of service to struggling schools around us as a "living out of gospel values in practice". Catholic schools should be known for their positive approach to partnership, with other Catholic schools, between state and independent schools, but also with non-Catholic schools that may need help.

The outward-facing posture called for by the Vatican Council also includes an openness to what is going on in the modern world. The *Pastoral Constitution on the Church in the Modern World* (*Gaudium et Spes*) put it strongly when it said that the Church has "a duty in every age of examining the signs of the times and interpreting them in the light of the Gospel, so that it can offer in a manner appropriate to each generation replies to the continual human questionings on the meaning of this life".[15] Today's Catholic educators feel this duty with more urgency than ever before. Our assemblies, liturgies, curriculum programmes and prayers should be engaged with the "signs of the times", the events and ideologies of the age, to help our students to answer those profound questions of meaning which haunt every generation.

In the next chapter I will consider one of the most pressing signs of the times, the conflict between jihadist ideology and the western world. We need to explore other trends in our society with our students and present them with a Gospel response. As we've noted already, we have a number of excellent groups

and agencies in the Church to help us in this work. The Catholic theatre group Ten Ten, for example, visits schools with compelling dramas on a range of modern topics, including the choices and consequences in relationships. In an age when marriage is on the decline and 42% of all marriages end in divorce,[16] we should be exploring with our students, many of whom will have gone through the pain of divorcing parents, how to sustain loving relationships in a marriage.

Our outward-facing stance should also be applied to developments in educational philosophy and practice. We can look for what is best in modern education and most in tune with our values and apply it in our schools.[17] One example is the work of Dr Carol Dweck of Stanford University on growth and fixed "mindsets". Dweck's Mindset approach is based on an understanding that intelligence *develops* over time. I have come across many students over the years who were convinced, or worse still, who had been convinced by others, that they were "rubbish at maths" or English, or PE – take your pick. This is a *fixed* mindset and is an educational disaster.

With a growth mindset, on the other hand, "people believe that their most basic abilities can be developed through dedication and hard work – brains and talent are just the starting point. This view creates a love of learning and a resilience that is essential for great accomplishment."[18] This is not the same as the facile version of the American Dream which says you can be anything you want to be, which is patently false. It is, however, an encouraging and supportive approach to learning that is backed by research and is well worth adopting. This approach is a good fit with the positive anthropology which should characterise a Catholic school, as well as with the Gospel value of hope (resilience).

5. Gospel Stewardship

The Gospel should not be reserved just for the religious aspects of the Catholic school. I have already referred to the very real danger of demoting Catholicity or the Gospel by consigning it to one department or colleague within the school: *the chaplain deals with that kind of thing*. John Sullivan points out that "as part of the Church, a Catholic school should bring the Gospel to bear on all aspects of its existence: the budget, timetable, resourcing, curriculum, pastoral care, and its internal and external relationships".[19] I am an English teacher by trade and when I started in headship I had not a clue about school finances or resources. I have been blessed throughout my time in headship with highly skilled bursars and they taught me all I needed to know about income and expenditure.

What I needed to bring to the discussion was the mission perspective: *are we spending our money in ways that are consistent with our Gospel values?* Take, as an example, vulnerable students to whom the Church "first and foremost"[20] offers its educational service. If we are attentive to the patterns of need among our students, especially some of the mental health needs identified in Chapter 1, and the increasingly complex special educational needs of our students, *is that reflected in the budget as a priority?* Do we have enough staff and the right kind of staff to meet their needs, or are we squeezing that budget to

pay for, say, marketing? It is ideal if everyone is asking that question, but if not, then the head teacher must take the lead. It is not enough to be content with a balanced budget and some money for your pet projects; you must carefully examine how time and money is spent in the school and test that against Gospel values.

There is another dimension of stewardship which John Sullivan brings to our attention – namely, that "we need not only convey the gospel, but also to receive it from others. For nobody 'possesses' the gospel in any secure or pure way. Our 'hold' on it is precarious and loosened, both collectively and individually, by sin."[21] This is a brilliant insight and one which anyone in a position of leadership in the Church should reflect upon. In the quotation from 2 Corinthians at the end of this chapter, we are reminded that we are the "clay jars" for this treasure, and sometimes we crack and the treasure seeps away. This should instil an attitude of humility in our leaders. We have suffered in the past from the arrogance of assuming that we possess the truth, but that attitude has been consigned to history.

If we proceed from a position of genuine humility, understanding that our "hold" on the Gospel is fragile, then we will be aware of the need to continually evangelise ourselves, never mind the need to evangelise anyone else. We should continually ask ourselves to what extent our operative values are any different to those of people who have no interest in the Gospel. To divert briefly from Luke's Gospel, there is a remarkable scene in Matthew's Gospel when a Canaanite woman challenges Jesus about his mission strategy. He is quite convinced that he was "sent only to the lost sheep of the house of Israel" (Matthew 15:24), but the woman's faith and perseverance convinces him to change his mind and cure her daughter. Jesus allowed his own understanding of the Gospel to be challenged by a woman he met along the way. We are merely stewards, asked to look after this treasure for a while, and we must never think it is ours or that we are properly in charge. There is a larger power at work, an "extraordinary power" (2 Corinthians 4:7), and our job more often than not is to get out of the way.

6. Servant Leader

The notion of servant leadership has gained a good deal of credibility in the business world following the work of Robert K. Greenleaf in response to what he saw as autocratic approaches to leadership in the business community of the 1970s. I consider Greenleaf's work and a Catholic interpretation of it by Sister Mary John Mananzan in *How to Survive in Leadership in a Catholic School*. For now, I would like to look briefly at how leadership is treated in the Gospels and share some of my own experience.

In Chapter 3 I identified humility as a Gospel value and referred to the scene at the last supper when, just as the mission seemed to be falling apart, the disciples were having a row about who was the greatest. There was clearly a lot about the ways of Jesus which took them a while to understand. They had been with him all that time and yet still didn't think that vying for positions of status was at odds with his teaching or example. This is a salutary point for leaders: it can take a long time to change a

culture, or "fixed" mindset. Jesus patiently refers to the standard leadership model of his day, which is kings lording it over their subjects, the way of Caesar. As one who says "follow me", he has taken quite a different approach. He reminds them that that he is among them "as one who serves" (Luke 22:27). Since some of them don't think this applies to them, he says that "the greatest among you must become like the youngest, and the leader like one who serves" (22:26).

So what might this look like for modern disciples in positions of leadership in Catholic schools? John Sullivan says that "in their use of authority, influence and power, Catholic school leaders should favour trust over control".[22] It is tempting when you are in headship to think you have to "win" all the time. Sullivan puts it well when he says that head teachers "should be concerned to win people over rather than simply win".[23] Now there may be times in the life of a school – when, for example, it is climbing out of an Ofsted category of Inadequate – when the "my way or the highway" approach might need to be adopted, but generally what is required is not the exercise of authority, but an authoritative approach to building a vision for the community which involves listening to people.

Head teachers must respect the accumulated wisdom of the community, but that does not mean that the school is a democracy. You can't take a vote on every decision. There is a role for a decision-maker. On many occasions in headship, having listened to the various views, the staff have looked to me to make a decision. Jesus made decisions, such as who to appoint as his twelve disciples. This has all the hallmarks of a historical event since it is so widely attested in the New Testament. What is striking in Luke's Gospel is that before he chose his twelve, "he spent the night in prayer to God" (Luke 6:12). We might now call this discernment, the need to reflect and pray about major moments in the life of a community. After another prayer experience, on the mountain of transfiguration, Jesus "set his face to go to Jerusalem" (Luke 9:51). Jesus in the Gospels is often seen as a driven figure. He is quite determined about the direction his mission has to take (some adjustments to strategy notwithstanding) and it is clear that the source of this determination is to be found in his prayerful union with the Father.

Another aspect of the ministry of Jesus which I touched on in Chapter 1 was his availability to people, even when he was emotionally and physically drained. At the heart of servant leadership in a Catholic school, inspired by our anthropology or understanding of the human person, should be time and space for one-to-one encounters. I remember once there was a knock on my office door five minutes before a staff briefing on a Monday morning, followed by, "Have you got a minute?" I made my impatience clear but said something like "Yes, but this will have to be quick." The teacher then told me about a close family member who had been diagnosed with terminal cancer. Her life was falling apart, she just needed some help. I felt ridiculously petty and stupid and gave her as much time as she needed, which wasn't much. She just needed to know I would support her. When I left the school years later she gave me a card and that moment in my office was what she thanked me for.

Leadership has always come with signs and symbols designed to reinforce status. That is very much the case today and we are still impressed by the individual who is driven around in the back of a big car with police outriders. Jesus consistently showed no interest in status symbols and promoted children as exemplars of the kingdom (Luke 18:17). There are many temptations in leadership, some more subtle than others, to enjoy your status. Sarah Conrad, in her leadership reflections at the end of this chapter, makes some telling points about the public signs of servant leadership in the school. It took me a few years to give up my reserved parking space, and that was only after David Wells spoke to the staff about Gospel leadership – after that, there was no going back. Sarah's point about the public display of staff photographs in reception is important. Does the head sit at the top with the staff ranged below her, or is it alphabetical? I made that change, but never got round to producing a servant leadership version of the whole school photograph. I've been in a few as head teacher, and always in the centre of the front row, frowning.

I mentioned earlier the importance of developing others in a spirituality of communion. A Catholic servant leader should see the spiritual development of others as a priority. I've said already that the community of a Catholic school will have people on a wide spectrum of faith commitment, from zero/estranged to the fully committed/practising. If a servant leader is led by the Spirit of God then he or she will take every opportunity to develop that Spirit in others, if they wish. Many schools now have chaplaincy or mission teams to encourage the spiritual development and leadership of their students. Increasingly, schools also have opportunities for staff prayer and formation, including what was always a highlight in my school, the annual staff training day devoted to spirituality. Those who are more open to spiritual formation in the school will not only help to maintain the "mission integrity" of the school by their witness, but they will act as a "leaven" in the school (a modest but transformational influence; see Luke 13:20–21), just as the school is a "leaven" in the wider society.

7. Think Well and Define Reality with Courage

Servant leadership should not be confused with servile leadership. Servant leaders are not doormats. You would not last five minutes in headship if your version of servant leadership involved letting people do what they want. Head teachers have to manage staff who are employed to do a job with expectations and objectives. When those people do not do their job properly they need to be held to account. Annie Sutton speaks to this point very powerfully in her reflections at the end of this chapter. In her school, where so many of the learners are damaged by their previous experiences in education, it is non-negotiable that their experience in her school is relentlessly positive. All staff have very clear expectations of how they should treat the learners. It is an excellent rationale for leadership in any school.

This point about accountability does not undermine anything I have said so far about Gospel values. Think of it this way: are you operating out of Gospel values if you allow your students to be badly taught and to pick up misconceptions in their knowledge, or if you see that their skills are being undeveloped, or that they are being subjected to unsafe or degrading treatment? No, that is not consistent with our anthropology. Where we see the Gospel values in action is in the way we treat the colleague who is being held to account. We treat them fairly and with compassion, respecting employment legislation, protecting their dignity, supporting them to do better, while calmly and clearly making the point that if nothing changes then they will have to leave.

Leadership styles have become very popular in recent years. When I was studying for the National Professional Qualification for Headship (NPQH), there was a great deal of emphasis on the different styles you might adopt in leadership to suit different situations: coercive, authoritative, affiliative, democratic, pacesetting and coaching. Coercive and pacesetting were found to have a consistently negative impact on climate, and coercive would certainly not be consistent with servant leadership. I found the work on leadership styles to be interesting for conference reflections but not much use on a Monday morning when I was back in school. A style does not really describe what you *do* in leadership. Sean Ruth, an Irish organisational psychologist, has developed a psychological approach to leadership which I find more useful. He says that "if there is one over-riding quality that is essential for leadership it is probably the ability to think well".[24]

I like this approach and have found it very helpful in recent years. If you ask yourself the question, "Who or what needs my *best thinking* this week?",[25] I have found that it helps to sharpen your attention on what is most important at that time. Ruth is not saying that the leader is the only one who should be thinking – far from it – but the leader is the one who facilitates the thinking, who taps into the thinking talent in the community. In my limited experience of doing school inspections, what characterised schools that were really struggling was the lack of clarity and coherence – *who is doing the thinking around here?* Or, *who has an understanding of the reality of this community?* Ruth says that "the ability of a leader to name or describe clearly what is happening is often a powerful resource for any group".[26] In the Gospels and in the Church we see that the naming or defining of reality is a key attribute of the kingdom of God.

In Luke's Gospel, Jesus does not hesitate to define the behaviour of the Pharisees for what it is from a kingdom perspective. When he is criticised by his host for not ritually washing before the meal, he retorts that the Pharisees "clean the outside of the cup and of the dish, but inside you are full of greed and wickedness" (Luke 11:39). This is not the kind of table talk you'd normally expect from your guests. Jesus bravely defines reality, with no regard for how he will be viewed as a result. We've seen similar courage from Pope Francis, who astonished the Roman Curia, the Church's government, at the Presentation of Christmas Greetings on 22 December 2014 in the Clementine Hall in Rome. Instead of the usual Christmas greetings, he went through fifteen "diseases in our life in the Curia".[27] Leadership does not help a community to grow and fulfil its mission by serving its members platitudes. Leadership sometimes has to stand up in front of them and tell it as it is, in ways best judged to help the community to improve or reform and then offer the vision to make things better.

Ruth makes the point that a key dimension of thinking well in leadership is to listen to other people, to really listen. This requires what he calls a "relaxed, deep, respectful" listening rather than a "pseudo-listening where the attention of the 'listener' is actually on their own thoughts, experiences or feelings".[28] When a leader listens to people in the community they have a better chance not only of helping them as individuals but of defining the reality of what is going on. Without that listening, the leader could make the fatal error of misreading the current situation, which will give rise to resentment and lack of support for the vision of what needs to be done. Pope Francis showed us an example of such listening in the 2014 and 2015 synods on the family. Rather than just restating the teaching of the Church, which some would have preferred, he invited comments from the faithful around the world and then opened up genuine discussion with the bishops.

8. Commitment to Excellence

The final sign of a Gospel-inspired leadership in a Catholic school is what I would define as a commitment to excellence in all areas. I have had many conversations over the years with head teachers and diocesan officers about the importance of exam results or daily standards in the school. If we are inspired by a Catholic anthropology and see in our students the image of the divine, then should we be overly concerned about exam results and whether or not the boys have their ties done up properly? Should we not just concentrate on the bigger picture of their formation as good and caring people rather than getting bogged down in superficial detail or subjecting them to exam stress? That question was answered for me when I took up my first headship in 2002.

The school was not in good shape: morale was low, behaviour was poor, and exam results were below what they should have been for the ability of the students. As a result, the local Catholic community had little confidence in the school. I did not live in the catchment area, but I remember at the time thinking that if I did I would not send my children there. The school was in "challenging circumstances" and was due a visit from HMI very soon, so we were in the "my way or the highway" mode rather than anything involving careful listening and discernment. Working on instinct and what I had learned from previous schools, I found money to build a trophy cabinet in reception, put down carpeting, wrote a behaviour policy and changed the uniform to blazers and ties. I was referring not to any handbook, but to an instinct that these students were not thriving in this environment and that their dignity and development would be better served with those changes. With support from staff, governors, students and parents we turned the school around and I'm pleased to say that due to subsequent good Catholic head teachers, the school has gone from strength to strength and is now over-subscribed.

The Church has never shown any hesitation when it comes to the importance of standards of education in Catholic schools. Canon Law states: "Directors of Catholic schools are to take care under the watchfulness of the local ordinary that the instruction which is given in them is at least as academically distinguished as that in the other schools of the area."[29] It is an interesting approach.

The Church cannot set an absolute standard for education, since that does not exist, but in relative terms, the quality of Catholic education should be measured against the best in the local area and not found wanting. The Bishops of England and Wales, in their most recent document, *Catholic Education in England and Wales* (2014), reaffirm their five distinctive features of Catholic education which were first outlined in the 1996 document, *Principles, Practices and Concerns*. The first of these is "the search for excellence", by which the school "strives to offer students every opportunity to develop their talents to the full through their academic work, spiritual worship and extracurricular activities".[30]

Excellence in all areas should be a characteristic of Catholic schools. The case for academic excellence has been made not only in terms of personal development but above all in terms of service of one's neighbour and the transformation of society. The case for daily standards is made in terms of the foundational anthropology of Catholic schools, which insists on the highest standards of care and behaviour to promote the dignity of the individual. Every other detail of the life of the school should be inspired by the same approach, whether it's the preparation for an assembly, an open evening or a staff meeting: has the best thinking been applied to this event, down to the smallest thoughtful detail? Some of this may seem far removed from the dusty villages of first-century Palestine, but if we stay focused on the values of Jesus we should avoid any temptation to slip into elitism or pride, which are both very far removed from the Gospel.

Reflections by Leaders in Catholic Education

The leaders, in their reflections on this topic, share the view that, in order to be authentic, Catholic head teachers need to be "practising" in the deepest sense of the word – to be followers of Jesus Christ, committed to a life of discipleship within the norms and practices of the Catholic Church. They also need to be tuned in to the reality of the lives of their staff and students, whose lived experience and guiding ideologies may be quite different to their own. There are some reflections here on headship as a vocation, a theme which I have not developed because I'm not convinced that headship is a vocation. Being a disciple of Jesus is a vocation, and in the course of a lifetime a disciple in the Church may be "called" to various apostolates. If we regard headship as a life's vocation, in the same way as priesthood or the religious life is, then what happens when you're no longer a head teacher? Is your life's vocation over?

◌

The State has, I think, a contradictory relation with Catholic schools. It esteems their general academic successes but it's disturbed by some of the counter-cultural values that Catholic schools are imparting to their students and it's obviously always in the interest of the State to reward and to focus on those things that the State values, which is the league table positions and so on. How can we preserve what I've called our "mission integrity"? That's what's at stake at the moment, our mission integrity. I think we won't be able to preserve the mission integrity of our schools if we do not have a significant number of the teachers within the school renewing their own spiritual capital, as I call it, their own sense of commitment to the Catholic religious mission so that they, all the time, are trying to be, like Thomas More, the king's good servant in so far as it is legitimate to be the king's good servant, but God's first. They can only do that if they've got internal spiritual strength, and where's that coming from? In the past we had a lot of vowed religious in charge of our schools. They'd had an extensive period of spiritual and moral formation. They had reserves of spiritual capital to draw on, but our current people are, as I've written, living on a declining asset. So the recent initiative, for instance, to introduce an annual national retreat for school leaders, and I hope for other teachers as well, that is essential because we shall not hold our mission integrity if we are not renewing the sources of mission integrity which must be some spiritual depth and commitment in the person.

—Professor Gerald Grace, Director of the Centre for Research and Development in Catholic Education, St Mary's, Twickenham

I suppose it's familiarity with the Gospel so that you can talk about that confidently and coherently, I think it's about an internalisation of that which is what I understand by spirituality so that it's not an "external rule" but it becomes your internal yardstick and inspiration. And then I think in a school context leadership then transfers from being something personal and private to something, not necessarily entirely, but something that is then public and publicly accessible because in the end it's going to be the example that you show. If people don't notice that your words and actions are coloured by the Gospel then you're a fraud, there's no authenticity to it. For a lot of people it will remain fairly external so their religion, their faith, is externally expressed at Mass or whatever it is. For a number they will then seriously internalise that and so they live out of that but then that going public, being willing to talk and stick by your principles when you're under flak because of that internalised Gospel, I think that's what you've got to do as a leader of a Christian community, certainly as a school leader, I'd have thought.

—Father Adrian Porter SJ, Delegate for Education for the British Province of the Society of Jesus

I believe that the values that we hold are actually universal values so I do think they speak to people at a level that is not simply labelling yourself a member of one faith or another, but far more than British values, I think the values that we hold to be true that come from the Gospels are actually about being human and I think because of that they do actually speak to people in some way. What shapes people is not what you tell them but what they see in practice. It's true for adults; it's true for children. What they see being modelled is what they take to be true about the school, so if you're going to show people what it means to live by the Gospel you

really have to model it for them. They have to see it in action. They have to believe that it is of value and that it doesn't threaten them or take away from their own individuality. Rightly or wrongly that does stem from the head. I think it's unfair on heads but I think what they model, where their priorities are, that determines the shape of the school.

—Diocesan Officer, Catholic Diocesan Education Department

The enormity of the role can sometimes overwhelm you; feeling pulled from one corner to another; trying to listen to so many sources of advice; grasping the responsibility of a cause built up by so many people in the parishes long before your time; remaining true to yourself and your vision. For this you need daily space, reflection and prayer, and as a new head I have found the encouragement of a spiritual director essential. This is a very different role from a mentor, SIP, family or friends who will always support you but may not ask those challenging questions about your vocation and the direction of your vision. I have been blessed and fortunate to have had one who has been there from day one offering spiritual guidance, a neutral perspective, time, questioning, reassurance and prayer.

—Clare Hogg, Head teacher, St Thomas More High School, Crewe

I think one sign of Gospel-inspired leadership in a Catholic school should be servant leadership. From my experience, people tend to go into leadership either because they feel drawn to it as a vocation or because they are after the power that comes with it, and I think Catholic leadership should be the first one. So I would want to see a real care for the young people we're teaching, a real care for staff and parents. The parent suffering from cancer, send them a little note or be there for them. I think that's really important, the way you treat others. I think you should be humble. When we put the *Who's Who in our School Community* up on the wall in reception, I wouldn't want me to be at the top. No, it should be in alphabetical order. I think that's really important.

I do give all new school staff a copy of *How to Survive Working in a Catholic School* and try and use bits of that in discussion as part of the induction because I do think it needs teasing out and I don't think it's just osmosis. I think it needs both and I think you need, as a leader, to be living it out so that they know you're walking the talk; but then if I did that and I didn't say explicitly *why* I was doing it, it would just be that I was a nice person.

—Sarah Conrad, Head of Prep School, St Teresa's, Effingham

I think you have to be an example for your staff. Talking about Gospel-inspired leadership, I think that's hugely important. I think, especially for a staff body where not many of them perhaps themselves are Catholic or certainly practising, I think they have to see what that looks like in reality and it has to be lived. And then being robust and very clear in your determination to do that because they

will probably be more vocal than the students at times in terms of whether they buy into that vision and they may feel that they're being asked to do something or that something's not important and I think it's just being absolutely clear and calm and saying this is what we're about. Whether it's educating the whole person or that we actually take time to do this and this takes priority. It goes right back to the idea of values, doesn't it? What's valuable to this community?

—Charlotte Cummins, Senior Deputy Head, Prior Park College, Bath

What I say is that actually I'm aggressively positive. It's non-negotiable, so our positive behaviour strategy extends to not only the learners but the staff as well. This is the only way and if you look at the ethos of the positive behaviour support, it's completely founded in Jesus' message. There's nothing there that contradicts it at all. That's then enshrined in policy, so, it's a strange thing to say, but, if you're not going to get on board with that positive approach I'm actually going to, at a particular level, hold you accountable for that. Every single individual has to be on board with that and that's laid out really clearly from the start and for some people it isn't the way for them, and if they can't change and they can't embrace it and they can't work with it, they have to leave. It really is very simple, so you're actually looking at a capability process because we have to be like this. The learners who come here, apart from about four in early years, have failed catastrophically in the mainstream. They've been expelled, it's all falling apart, it's been a hideous experience for them. Probably multiple times before they finally end up here. We can't say that simply by putting them in twenty-three acres with all our staff and all our facilities that this is going to fix them. So when they come here we have to, for everybody's survival, do something fundamentally different to what's gone on before, and if you don't buy in to that, if you think that the waggy finger and the "You will!" is going to work, you have to learn really quickly that it doesn't and if you refuse to learn you have to move on. I should add that we lose very few people because they don't agree with the positive approach.

—Anne Sutton, Executive Principal, St Joseph's Special School, Cranleigh

I come back to the point about implicit and explicit, a discussion in an academic setting about *Laudato Si'* opens up and brings you towards Gospel values – respect, solidarity, love – but if you were to basically take those in abstract form and try to educate individuals about them there could be resistance, a turn off. But contextualising them for our employees in this city who would be finding it very difficult to find housing, some of their children will be worried about their future and the whole finding of work and sustainable work, now there is a touch point where you are meeting people on the basis of their real human concerns and you're saying to them, "Here's a moral and societal framework coming out of a different tradition which is

offering to your society a menu or a recipe that might be considered as part of a solution." So, I've always found the encyclicals to be that touch point which helps you in the world because it's about knowing the challenges you face.

—Francis Campbell, Vice-Chancellor of St Mary's University, Twickenham

A new head comes in and says we can pull the academic performance up, we need to do this, this and this, and the staff say, "That's not what we're about. We care for these children." I think the idea is that actually caring for them is pushing them to do their very best academically. Going back to that, live your life fully to be the person you can be is pushing young people to see that within the Christian faith academic success can be part of that. And then it comes to how do you interpret, are we doing academic success so we can go to Oxford and Cambridge and earn lots of money or are we doing it because we can fulfil our purpose in the world, our vocation in the world? If you understand your life as a vocation, which you would do within a Catholic context, then academic success is part of that vocation.

If leadership embodies those values and virtues then you're talking about leadership that can have an effect on a Catholic school. It cannot be an individual though. I think looking at the examples that I've looked at, you can't say an individual can come in and we can make this a Catholic school … you've got to have other people on board. So if you have the idea that yes, this is my vision, but it's got to be our vision and it's got to be that idea of leadership within the framework of the Christian faith. Talking to a lot of leaders of Christian schools, when they're talking to me they're talking about vocation. Even though they might not use the word "vocation", a lot of it is about God's purpose for me, and then how do I live out God's purpose. And if you're constantly reflecting that what you're doing is God's purpose then I think that leadership can only be a reflective leadership and it can be quite different. It's not to say there's one sort of leadership that works for Catholic schools but you can see a variety of approaches, but always that sense of reflection. I'm reflecting on what I'm doing and I'm doing this because I believe.

—Dr Ann Casson, Research Fellow at National Institute for Christian Education Research (NICER), Canterbury Christ Church University

My distinctive take on the Beatitudes is centring around the concept of singleness of purpose, and this is about leadership really. You can see that threaded through the sermon, so I start with this "Blessed are the pure in heart for they shall see God." I think that's been confused with secularly pure, all those kind of things. Whereas my view based on biblical scholarship is that we're not talking about that here; these pure in heart people are people with a clear vision. So that has important resonances with leadership, so does other parts of the sermon in Matthew, like 5:48, "Be perfect as your heavenly Father is perfect." Theologically, only one is perfect, and that's God, so here the word used is *teleos*, and that means more like consistently, singleness of purpose, integrity, holiness, much like the "narrow gate", whereas the "wide gate" in leadership terms is being seduced by whatever comes along.

—Dr John Lydon, Programme Director for Catholic School Leadership, at St Mary's University, Twickenham

I don't think it works unless the leader really lives the life, spiritual life, has a regular prayer life and buys into it at that deep level. I think you could do that and still be a poor leader because you haven't got other skills, but I think that, as it were, the "complete" Catholic leader does need to have that and I think that you can have people who are more nominally Catholic who can learn it, but if it's learnt from the outside it won't really infuse leadership properly and that's why I think sometimes it can be that somebody who has a living faith might be a better Catholic leader than somebody who is a Catholic but not really living it.

—Stephen Oliver, Principal, Our Lady's Abingdon

Reflections from Scripture

But we have this treasure in clay jars, so that it may be made clear that this extraordinary power belongs to God and does not come from us. We are afflicted in every way, but not crushed; perplexed, but not driven to despair; persecuted, but not forsaken; struck down, but not destroyed. (2 Corinthians 4:7–9)

All this is from God, who reconciled us to himself through Christ, and has given us the ministry of reconciliation; that is, in Christ God was reconciling the world to himself, not counting their trespasses against them, and entrusting the message of reconciliation to us. So we are ambassadors for Christ, since God is making his appeal through us; we entreat you on behalf of Christ, be reconciled to God. (2 Corinthians 5:18–20)

But I do not count my life of any value to myself, if only I may finish my course and the ministry that I received from the Lord Jesus, to testify to the good news of God's grace. (Acts of the Apostles 20:24)

On their return the apostles told Jesus all they had done. He took them with him and withdrew privately to a city called Bethsaida. When the crowds found out about it, they followed him; and he welcomed them, and spoke to them about the kingdom of God, and healed those who needed to be cured. (Luke 9:10–11)

Further Reading for Gospel-inspired Leaders

Enzo Bianchi, *Lectio Divina* (London: SPCK, 2015)

Pope Francis, *The Joy of the Gospel* (London: Catholic Truth Society, 2013)

Raymond Friel, *How to Survive in Leadership in a Catholic School* (Chawton: Redemptorist Publications, 2015)

Thomas Keating, *Open Mind, Open Heart: the contemplative dimension of the Gospel* (London: Bloomsbury, 2006)

Richard Rohr, *Immortal Diamond* (London: SPCK, 2013)

Sean Ruth, *Leadership and Liberation: a psychological approach* (Hove: Routledge, 2006)

CHAPTER 6

Forming Good Citizens:
notes towards a civilisation of love

– CHAPTER 6 –

Forming Good Citizens:
notes towards a civilisation of love

Fundamental British Values

Chapter 1 looked at the background to the government's use of fundamental British values as a way to measure radicalisation in schools. With the growing threat of terrorism at home and evidence that young people from this country were being radicalised and travelling to Syria to join terrorist groups, the Home Secretary launched the Prevent Strategy in June 2011. In the education section, as noted previously, it said that a small number of independent faith schools had been promoting views that were contrary to British values. The Catholic Education Service (CES) has produced a briefing paper entitled "Catholic Values and 'British Values': the background to the debate on 'British values'" (2015). While the paper provides a helpful summary of the origins of fundamental British values and the Prevent Strategy, it does not in fact describe Catholic values and the extent to which they may or may not coincide with British values.

Another CES paper issued around the same time, "Catholic Values and 'British Values': practical advice from the Catholic Education Service", contained a statement for Catholic schools to use on their websites to clarify their educational purpose, especially regarding a broad and balanced curriculum and a commitment to British values, as follows:

> This is a Catholic school which seeks to live out the values of Jesus Christ. We promote these values by our words and deeds, and Catholic doctrine and practice therefore permeates every aspect of the school's activity. We provide a Catholic curriculum, which is broad and balanced, recognising that every pupil is unique and created in the image of God (Gen 1:27). Our curriculum is designed to enable every pupil to discern their vocation and to be well-equipped to follow it as active citizens in service of the world. Catholic Religious Education is the "core of the core curriculum" (Pope St John Paul II) and the foundation of the entire educational process. We also provide a wide range of extra-curricular activities and strong pastoral support. We incorporate democratic principles, value the rule of law, support individual liberty and foster a community in which different faiths and beliefs are respected.[1]

Some of the "signs" we have identified as typical of a

Gospel-inspired school can be seen here, such as the dignity of pupils made in the image of God and the importance of vocation, service, extra-curricular activities and pastoral support. The values of Jesus Christ are mentioned in the first sentence but they are taken as read rather than spelled out. The point that was considered in some detail in Chapter 4 about the curriculum is described in terms of "Catholic doctrine and practice" permeating every aspect of the school's activity. This goes beyond what was envisaged in *The Catholic School*, which was a curriculum with content delivered "in the light of the Gospel".[2]

The briefing paper also provides some helpful suggestions for how Catholic schools, maintained and independent, can fulfil their duty to promote each of the fundamental British values. I have taken the suggestions and added some additional points:

Democracy

* Having a school council with elected representatives, which encourages a genuine student voice

* Taking part in debating competitions internally or with other schools and ensuring that open debate is part of the culture in the classroom

* Using history lessons and assemblies to highlight the struggle for democratic systems and the harm done by totalitarian regimes

* Voting in the school for pupil leadership roles such as Head Boy/Girl in ways which encourage substantial discussion rather than a popularity contest

* Inviting MPs, local councillors and other speakers to the school who will not undermine the school's ethos

* Visiting the Houses of Parliament, local town halls or councils

* Holding mock elections or referenda while reminding the staff that they must observe political neutrality

* Participating in the UK Youth Parliament or any other local youth forum.

The Rule of Law

* Involving students in drafting the school behaviour policy which has a clear foundation in Gospel values

* Arranging visits from the police and other agencies to reinforce the key messages about public order and consequences

* Highlighting the rules of the Church and the tradition of natural law in RE and assemblies, including the foundational importance of the Ten Commandments and the New Law of the Sermon on the Mount

* Teaching about the development of the rule of law in English law, a legal system created in a

Catholic England, inspired by Christian values, and an influence across the world

Individual Liberty

- Encouraging students to be independent in their learning with a "growth" mindset, taking responsibility for their learning

- Developing a culture of vocation with opportunities for reflection and discernment, and with examples of inspirational lives throughout the curriculum

- Fostering a culture committed to equality, based on the foundational anthropology of the school and observant of legislation such as the Equality Act 2010.

Mutual Respect

- Embedding a culture of respect and courtesy in the school, including a culture of respect for the opinions of others in lessons and debates

- Promoting an effective anti-bullying and anti-racism policy and involving the students in reviewing impact

- Emphasising in RE and PSHE education the foundational belief in the dignity of the individual

- Encouraging partnerships with other schools and religious communities, which fosters respect

- Promoting works of mercy and a culture committed to social justice.

Tolerance of those with Different Faiths and Beliefs

- Raising pupils' awareness of the faith and traditions of other religious communities in order to respect and understand them, as stated in the *Religious Education Curriculum Directory* (2012)

- Highlighting how the view of the Church regarding other faiths and beliefs has evolved up to the Second Vatican Council's *Nostra Aetate* ("Declaration on the Relationship of the Church to Non-Christian Religions")

- Highlighting the levels of openness Jesus showed in the Gospels to those from other faiths and beliefs (e.g. the Samaritan woman at the well [John 4:4–26] and eventually the Canaanite woman [Matthew 15:21–28])!

In recent years, when the State wanted to influence the behaviour or beliefs of young people, schools were asked to make changes to their curriculum and then the monitoring agents of the State were called upon to ensure that the changes were being implemented. The promotion of British values was included in a revised Ofsted framework and in revised Independent School Standards. In the *School Inspection Handbook* (2015), any school that aspired to achieve a grade of Outstanding for Leadership and Management (and Canon 806 could be interpreted as an injunction from the Church to be Outstanding, depending on local circumstances) needed to show, among other things, that "pupils' spiritual, moral, social and cultural development and, within this, the promotion of fundamental British values, are at the heart of the school's work".[3] This is one of twelve bullet points in the grade descriptors for Outstanding and inspectors apply a "best fit" when forming a final judgement, but it does raise a challenging question for Catholic schools. To what extent should British values be "at the heart of the school's work"? In reality, school inspectors are not generally inclined to be pedantic unless a serious issue has been flagged up, but nevertheless an answer is required.

There is a line of argument in Catholic education, which we can see from some of the reflections of our leaders at the end of this chapter, that Gospel values pre-date and subsume British values. The crossover, however, is not tidy. As some of our leaders point out, there are aspects of the law which contradict the teaching of the Church. The British value of tolerance is held by many to be weak and unhelpful in comparison with the Gospel values of compassion and love. These tensions for the time being are in the background and any inspection team in the course of less than two days in a school would have to be quite determined to bring them to the surface. In the meantime, it is in our interests to show how we promote British values within the context of our Gospel values. In my last headship we developed the tag line "Inspired by Gospel Values, Promoting British Values" for our website slider announcing the assembly theme of the week. It is one way of expressing the advice of Jesus not to go to war with Caesar (see scripture reflections at the end of Chapter 1) or Thomas More's dictum that we are

"the king's good servants, but God's first".

Our Gospel inspires us to go beyond the conventional and is, as many of our leaders have said, counter-cultural. The Catechism of the Catholic Church refers to the "Law of the Gospel"[4] which fulfils (rather than replaces) the Old Law. This New Law "is the work of Christ and is expressed particularly in the Sermon on the Mount"[5] (Matthew's version is preferred in the Catechism). The purpose of the New Law is to "reform the heart, the root of human acts".[6] It practises the *acts of religion* which are almsgiving, prayer and fasting. It is called a law of love, grace and freedom, because it "inclines us to act spontaneously by the prompting of charity".[7] It changes our relationship to God from that of a servant who doesn't know what is going on "to that of a friend of Christ".[8] It is essentially about "love of God and neighbour",[9] and neighbour includes our enemy. Even the Catechism refers to "the surprising ways of the Kingdom".[10] The human beings who have been asked to witness to this law are as flawed as any other human beings (in fact, what marks out Christians is that they know they are flawed), but the law that we strive to observe, while it contradicts what much of the world believes, is not against the world. Its foundation is love, the good of others.

As a Church we have become better at acknowledging our flaws in recent years, as have many other institutions. While we agree to promote the government's rule of law, we also need to recognise that as a Catholic community we have a memory of that law working against us. In a very powerful testimony at the end of this chapter, Francis Campbell reminds us that if you were a Catholic living in Northern Ireland in the 1970s or 80s then you may have struggled to support or promote the rule of law and British values, since so much of that law seemed to be discriminatory. He also develops the compelling thesis that one of the reasons why the conflict was not worse (very bad as it was) was because Catholic schools and the Catholic Church did not radicalise the population or promote violence.

In the example he gives of the republican Eamon Collins, there is a grim irony in the fact that he was radicalised to kill the agents of the British State by an English Marxist academic in a state-funded university. In more recent times, we have seen the struggle of the families and friends of those killed in the Hillsborough disaster in 1989 to achieve justice in the face of obstruction from agents of the law. In the end, the law did side with the truth, but only because of their determined efforts. The rule of secular law is not an absolute, nor is it always consistent with the teaching of the Church, and the agents of that law, like some representatives of the Church, have at times been found badly wanting. Nevertheless, we proceed with the faith that law is necessary for the good of society, and what we can bring to the discourse is that law based on the Gospel (the New Law) will protect human dignity and promote human flourishing.

Prevent Duty

In 2015, the government extended the reach of the law into schools with the passing of the Counter Terrorism and Security Bill. This new legislation requires all schools "to prevent people from being drawn into terrorism".[11] On the face of it, the aim of the legislation seems reasonable. Everything about our schools, as I have said from the beginning, is against violence and hatred, and we would not wish to see any of our students being drawn to the "calling" of terrorism. If a culture of vocation is rooted in a desire to serve others, then terrorism is a perverse vocation. However, as you will see from the comments of several of our Catholic leaders at the end of this chapter, there are serious misgivings about the extent of the Prevent Duty. It is not unreasonable to conduct risk assessments, arrange staff training, or open up debate among the students on extremism, but schools in addition are required to "make referrals if they are concerned that an individual might be vulnerable to radicalisation".[12] In other words, schools are being asked to be "surveillance agents", to use Gerald Grace's phrase, and that is a source of profound anxiety.

Cardinal Vincent Nichols, in an address to Catholic head teachers in 2015, referred to those young people who are vulnerable to radicalisation as "clean skins" who are as yet "unformed by substantive values".[13] He highlighted the role of social media as the recruiting tool of choice for the extremists. They are tapping into a desire in the vulnerable for connection, information, guidance, entertainment and a cause to follow. It is a timely reminder to Catholic leaders to be attentive to these "signs of the times" and to make every effort to understand social media and the platforms used by the students. Cardinal Nichols reminds us of our responsibility to take seriously the Church's call to develop a culture of vocation. We will not be serving humanity, he said, if we lack "the courage to present, explore and develop a vision which is going to grip a young life and act as a point of integration and meaning for all that will occur".[14] He reminds us of the central role of vocation in our schools – that there is "a personal vocation from God for every person given the gift of life by God".[15] In such a fruitful environment, we will help our young people to find their place in the world and "see themselves as gifted contributors to a wide and embracing vision of truth and purpose".[16]

Cardinal Nichols is drawing on a long tradition in the Church of commitment to the good of humanity. The first papal encyclical on Christian education that I'm aware of is *Spectata Fides* ("Outstanding Faith"), written by Pope Leo XIII to the Bishops of England in 1885. He commends the newly restored hierarchy for providing schools for their children. Reflecting more widely on the purpose of Catholic schools, the Pope goes on to say that "it is by these schools that good citizens are brought up for the State; for there is no better citizen than the man who has believed and practised the Christian faith from his childhood".[17] There we have our first modern statement on the *service* Catholic schools offer to society ("*for* the State"). In a comment that would apply with equal force today, the Pope says to the bishops that "very many of your nation are not a little anxious about religious education".[18] He reminds them that society needs Christian wisdom and urges them to make "the young your chief care".[19]

The next and most recent papal encyclical on Christian education was *Divini Illius Magistri* ("On the Christian Education of Youth") from Pope Pius XI in 1929. In a context of nascent fascism in Europe, the letter is concerned to establish the rights and responsibilities of parents to educate their children in the faith and of the Church to fulfil this aspiration of parents. There is a focus on original sin, which we have largely lost in recent years. The letter insists that "every method of education founded, wholly or in part, on the denial of original sin and of grace, and relying solely on the powers of human nature, is unsound".[20] In our day-to-day work with staff, children and teenagers, it is salutary to remind ourselves that we are dealing with fragile human nature which is inclined to "weakness of will and disorderly affections"[21] without the grace of God to help us to live according to the New Law. We may call this "old-fashioned" language, but it is a helpful corrective to an idealistic version of our anthropology which may end up thinking that our children can do no wrong.

The letter provides several examples of the Church's attitude to the State. In a rhetorical challenge to those who say that the teaching of Christ is opposed to the welfare of the State, Pius XI says "give us subjects, husbands, wives, parents, children, masters, servants, kings, judges, taxpayers and tax gatherers who live up to the teachings of Christ; and then let them dare assert that Christian doctrine is harmful to the State".[22] Ten years later, the question would have to be asked about the relation of the Christian to the fascist State, a question answered powerfully by some of our exemplars of Gospel values in Chapter 3 and also by Vatican II's commentary on conscience and justice. Pius XI takes us as far back as Tertullian, writing at the beginning of the third century, to show that we have always been contributors to society: "We take shop [sic] with you and we serve in your armies; we are farmers and merchants with you; we interchange skilled labour and display our works in public for your service. How can we seem unprofitable to you with whom we live and of whom we are, I know not."[23] If anything we have come too far along the path of assimilation, and perhaps we don't stand out enough from the mainstream, which is why Pope Francis is calling us out of our comfort zone.

We have been asked by the State to develop and demonstrate skills and attitudes that will allow our students to "participate in and contribute to life in modern Britain".[24] The State does not articulate with any confidence what those skills and attitudes are beyond a broad aspiration that young people have employment and opportunities. We've seen in recent years the use of the language of character, but mostly confined to the "performance" virtues of resilience, collaboration and perseverance. The values of modern Britain have been defined in ways which raise many questions, not least in terms of their provenance and the extent to which they actually describe the operative values of the population.

As we've seen from the Church documents, we have always been committed to the good of the body politic. Our schools are part of a tradition which will always work to provide our students with the skills and attitudes to participate in and contribute to society but which will always seek to go further: to develop values that are inspired by the Gospel which will encourage our students to be citizens who serve others and have a particular care for the vulnerable. If we really wanted to be controversial we could say that we *are* seeking to radicalise our students, since the Gospel we are promoting is a radically different view of reality from the mainstream, but it would take a confident and converted leader to articulate the mission in that way.

Civilisation of Love

There are many voices now being heard in our society arguing for an end to faith schools. For them, the Trojan Horse controversy in Birmingham is a useful means to label all faith schools as extremist and divisive. The Archbishop of Canterbury, Justin Welby, has said that "commentary around 'Trojan Horse' has made it sound as if schools with a religious character are a problem. That's simply not true and that fact seems to need a lot of repeating: no church schools or faith-based schools were caught up in 'Trojan Horse'."[25] The Chief Inspector's report in June 2014 stated that in some schools governors had attempted to "impose and promote a narrow faith-based ideology".[26] All the schools involved were community schools, not faith schools, but phrases like "narrow faith-based ideology" are happily picked up by the secular lobby and used against all faith schools.

Chapter 1 looked briefly at one of a number of reports which have questioned the role of faith schools. *Living with Difference*, published by the Woolf Institute, Cambridge, in 2015, not only called for a national conversation about fundamental values but also, among its twelve recommendations, included one stating that "bodies responsible for admissions and employment policies in schools with a religious character ('faith schools') should take measures to reduce selection of pupils and staff on grounds of religion".[27] If this were to happen it would seriously undermine the nature of our Catholic schools as described in Chapters 4 and 5. Without "practising" Catholics who are inspired by the Gospel, the distinctive nature of our schools would disappear and we would fade into the general marketplace of education, which is exactly what opponents of faith education want. We must develop in our leaders the confidence to articulate what we stand for, not in the old adversarial way, but in a hope-filled and Gospel-inspired way which insists that we are a benefit to society and have every reason to continue to exist.

The 2013 document from the Congregation for Catholic Education entitled *Educating to Intercultural Dialogue in Catholic Schools: living in harmony for a civilization of love* (hereafter *Educating to Intercultural Dialogue*) considers the attempts by the wider secular lobby to exclude religion from the public square. It shows how, in a similar way to Trojan Horse in Britain, the rise of violent Islamic fundamentalism is used to label all religious groups as anti-liberal, superstitious and divisive. Religion belongs in the private sphere, the argument runs, and has no place in public discourse and public life. Reason will guide us rather than the "hocus pocus" of religion. Arguing against this, however, the document says that "the exclusion of religion from the public square … hinders an encounter between persons and their collaboration for the progress of humanity".[28] It makes the point that human rights would be in danger of being ignored if religion were omitted from the discourse because those rights could be "robbed of their transcendent foundation or because personal freedom is not acknowledged".[29] It also rejects the

claim that there can be no fruitful dialogue between reason and religious faith. The view of the Church, based on the work of Thomas Aquinas, is that "reason always stands in need of being purified by faith … religion always needs to be purified by reason".[30]

Rupert Shortt provides an overview of the current anti-religious sentiment in *God is No Thing*. He confirms what was said in Chapter 1 – that religion is being written out of the script. He quotes the example of an article by the journalist Bryan Appleyard. He is discussing the work of American novelist Marilynne Robinson but comes to the sticking point that the main theme of her work is religion, which "many, probably most, British people – artists, writers, audiences – will find exotic because to them, religion has been embarrassed out of existence".[31] Appleyard clearly assumes that the polemical atheists, such as Dawkins, Hitchens, *et al.*, have won the day and religion has been consigned to the museum of curiosities. Shortt and others have put up a robust argument that this is far from the case.

Educating to Intercultural Dialogue goes on to emphasise the need for intercultural and interreligious dialogue. As the global temperature rises, both literally and emotionally, it seems that the voice of the Church has become more and more focused on the heart of its mission rather than engaging in aggressive polemic. In an age when the fundamentalists are seeking to ignite a war of civilisations, the Church insists that "dialogue, the fruit of knowledge, must be cultivated for people to co-exist and build up a civilization of love".[32] The aim of this dialogue is to reduce tension and conflict and increase knowledge and mutual understanding, which in turn reduces ignorance and misconception. We are being asked to take a step beyond merely the study of other faiths and cultures to personal encounter and the building of friendships. Catholic schools are well placed for this kind of mission. The broader purpose of Catholic schools in this new world of global community and conflict, at grave risk from superficiality, greed and fundamentalism, is spelled out with great clarity:

Catholic schools are encouraged to promote a wisdom-based society, to go beyond knowledge and educate people to think, evaluating facts in the light of values. They educate people to take on responsibility and duties, and exercise active citizenship…

The curriculum must help the students reflect on the great problems of our time, including those where one sees more clearly the difficult situation of a large part of humanity's living conditions. These would include the unequal distribution of resources, poverty, injustice and human rights denied. "Poverty" implies a careful consideration of the phenomenon of globalization, and suggests a broad and developed vision of poverty, in all its forms and causes.[33]

The more I study the Church's teaching on education, the more I come to regard it as something like a symphonic piece of music. A number of key themes or motifs recur and interweave over the years: dignity, service, citizenship, the poor, vocation, community, justice. If there is one central theme, or melody line, then it is the figure of Jesus, the vulnerable name for God, the revelation of mercy and love. This is what we have to offer our children and young people: an education according to a vision of reality which regards love as the destiny of every human being, "the goal of life itself".[34] We are committed to forming citizens of the world who will take their place in the twenty-first century as ambassadors of compassion and reconciliation, agents of transformational change who are smart enough to see how injustice works and how wrongs can be righted. This is our offer to the world and it's not bad.

There are those committed to the other "way" of death and mayhem in the name of a god that we do not recognise or in the name of a twisted ideology of racial hatred. We must remember that the extremism we have been asked to prevent is not just Islamic extremism, it is also right-wing hatred. In the face of such violence we do not respond with violence. That is not the way of Jesus. We work patiently and with perseverance for the good. Thousands of Christians have been killed by extremists in recent years in the Middle East, Asia and North Africa, but the killing of one elderly priest in northern France on 26 July 2016 graphically showed the vulnerability of the Church. Fr Jacques Hamel was saying Mass in the church at Saint-Étienne-du-Rouvray when two young men claiming to be ISIS militants arrived on a mission of death. They made the old priest kneel down and killed him by slitting his throat before they themselves died in a hail of police bullets.

The response of the Church to this horrific attack has provided powerful witness to the wider world about what we stand for. Monsignor Olivier Ribadeau Dumas, the secretary general of the French Bishops' Conference, said: "We want to maintain and develop dialogue between the different people in our country. We need peace, we need fraternity, we need to build a society where people love each other, and we will continue on this path. We should see the horizon, the horizon of peace, of joy, brotherhood and prayer. We are rooted in our faith and in Christ and we believe that evil and violence will not have the upper hand."[35] Archbishop Dominique Lebrun of Rouen said after the attack, "The Catholic Church has no other weapons besides prayer and fraternity between men."[36] Our path is the way of Jesus, who did not come to start a war of civilisations, but showed us how to work towards the civilisation of love.

Reflections by Leaders in Catholic Education

In the comments from Catholic leaders on the question of British values and the Prevent Strategy, there were strong views about the provenance of these values. A number felt that they had no real foundations other than political expediency. There were serious concerns about the tension between promoting the rule of law and the teaching of the Church, but there is an underlying assumption that we are "canny" enough not to run into open conflict with monitoring authorities on this issue. There were concerns about the Prevent Strategy, not in principle, but in the demand that schools refer students who

are causing concern. As always, there was positive engagement, and a number of leaders saw in the Prevent Strategy an opportunity to highlight and extend the work they do on other religions, open up even wider debate on issues of global concern, and above all promote the Gospel message of love and reconciliation which is our great offer to society.

᨟

There are very few cardinal rules within political science, there are one or two. One is, democracies don't go to war with each other – by and large it's true. The second is that when religion is a variable in a conflict, it's automatically a high-intensity conflict in terms of casualties, and Northern Ireland is an exception to that second rule because religion clearly was a variable, it may not have been a dominant variable but it was certainly a variable in the conflict but yet, comparatively, that conflict was not high intensity in terms of victims. A lot of people died and a lot of people were injured but when you look at it comparatively with international relations it was over a forty-year period, it didn't tip into civil war and when you look and ask why, there are a number of arguments that could be used and one of them would be the role of the Catholic Church and in particular the role of Catholic schools.

Catholics were the main secessionist group. They were the ones with the difficulty with the State. There was a strong sense of alienation, but Catholic schools were the places where the debate was taken on. So how did you avoid young people being radicalised? That was primarily the role of the teachers where debate was taking place within the school. A whole plethora of state initiatives around confidential telephone numbers and all that sort of stuff advertised every evening on the television, everywhere, every child of a certain age would know the number but the police or army or apparatus of the State was never brought into the Catholic schools, could never come in to the Catholic schools to start articulating a security response because that State had no credibility to say it.

People were refraining from it because of a Christian morality, and this was illustrated for me very, very clearly in a book that was published in 1998 called *Killing Rage* by a senior figure in the Irish Republican Army who was since murdered, called Eamon Collins. In that book he says that his radicalisation up to the point that he started killing for the republican cause came at the secular university in Belfast and it came at the hands of an English academic who was committed to Marxism. That was who radicalised him. In the book, he said, "I found for the first time a legitimisation for killing for the cause that my Irish nationalist Catholic upbringing had prevented me from doing and despite the fact," he said, "that from my mother I had inherited a Nationalist Republican reading of history, the Catholic morality, the Catholic framework had consistently taught me that killing for the cause was wrong."

Had I looked and seen somebody articulating British values of democracy and respect for the law and justice, I would have seen a set of contradictions since I was second class. The entity that contributed most to my understanding of being able to participate in this society confidently, openly and to engage within society was what I took from Gospel values because that's where I saw them being authentically lived out. It would have been much easier for some of those teachers or some of those clergy in the parishes to have gone with the popular mood, to have tapped into resentment or alienation and pushed us all over a cliff, but they didn't, they held fast to something much deeper and I think the same can be said in relation to the mainstream protestant churches.

—Francis Campbell, Vice-Chancellor, St Mary's University, Twickenham

It is understandable that the British State wants to try to prevent the development of forms of extremism in our schools but I simply think the use of school teachers as surveillance agents in their relations with students is going to be very counter-productive because what is the essential base of teacher/student relations, especially in the teenage adolescent years? It's got to be that of some mutual trust, and this policy, it seems to me, where they know that the teachers are acting as surveillance agents for the State, is going to undermine that trust and I think obviously there has to be surveillance agents looking for signs of extremism but it should not, in my view, be the teachers in the schools. It should be external agencies and my own view is it is the fundamental responsibility of individual families and parents to be monitoring their children and not school teachers. I think it's quite wrong to have brought the school teachers in as State agents.

—Professor Gerald Grace, Director of the Centre for Research and Development in Catholic Education, St Mary's, Twickenham

You never get any justification for where those values come from. They were just presented as British values but there's no sense of where do those values come from for us as a community. And values can't be plucked out of the air and offered to people like that, they have to come from somewhere, they have to be rooted in something. When you think of the one that's listed as the British values as tolerance, but I don't like that at all, the key word should be respect – for others. Because respect implies dialogue whereas tolerance indicates distance. I think it should be respect. But when you look at Church documents the protection of the individual is enshrined in Church documents, the need to respect individuals. It's the whole of who we are because we believe that each individual is created as a child of God because God is part and parcel of you, part and parcel of me, part and parcel of everybody else. I cannot not respect them. I cannot not wish to know more about them. I cannot not wish to dialogue with them, and that doesn't come from my Britishness, that comes from the core of who I am, my faith. That is ingrained in everything that we are as a community. It's not just Catholic social teaching, it's before that, it's

the very essence of what we believe about humanity.

—Diocesan Officer, Catholic Diocesan Education Department

You could say they're the values of any democratic society, and I think that raises a question for some young people as to why they're British. The same thing happens with the Gospel values/Catholic values, that you can get a view that, these are Catholic values and we're Catholic, we've got these values. Those others out there, outside that fold, haven't got these values. Which again is dangerous because a lot of the Gospel values or the Christian values are also values that are common across a lot of religions and it's just putting that boundary up which is not always helpful.

Radicalisation or preventing radicalisation is about education, and if you're educated in the values and you have a strong sense of your own opinion, which is often what children say in RE, "I can form my opinion." And they're forming their opinion in a safe space where the teacher's really got control but they don't realise that yet, they think they're free to say anything, and they can work out from informed sources what they think. Schools can do a lot to prevent radicalisation through education and through enabling young people to see things for what they are, rather than shutting down a conversation so the students [have] to look elsewhere.

—Dr Ann Casson, Research Fellow at National Institute for Christian Education Research (NICER), Canterbury Christ Church University

I believe that political agendas such as British Values and Every Child Matters are watered-down versions of what Catholic schools have been promoting for many years. However, in a multi-cultural school it is vital that British values are discussed, explored and debated but constantly reminding ourselves, and outside agencies, that the inclusive and accepting Gospel values will always take the lead. I would expect a Catholic school to work closely with all their families and parishes to ensure the safety of all, working with agencies, to ensure the Prevent Duty is implemented. The Prevent Duty needs to be dealt with sensitively and without bias, with the safety of the child as paramount. In this unsettled time Catholic schools need to break down barriers to allow open conversations and trust with their families.

—Clare Hogg, Head teacher, St Thomas More Catholic High School, Crewe

What we will do is we'll work with the young person for them to get an understanding of the social concepts around what they've done because we are trying to equip them to live in society and what they need to understand is, even if they don't understand why, they need to understand that in order to get along there are certain things you just can't do and it doesn't matter if you've got a learning disability. If you break the law, you break the law. Over 40% of the people who are currently in prison at the moment have a diagnosed learning disability, diagnosed, and that's really quite terrifying, isn't it? A very

high proportion, and I wonder about that cohort that are in prison with a learning disability, and I think of some of our learners here and we have a real fear that that's actually where they'll end up because they're not able to deal with the more complex elements of language and communication, and to the untrained eye they're going to come across as somebody who's a bit odd and possibly a bit aggressive and rather rude and that's going to get you into trouble, so we have to support those type of learners especially. They're the ones who are most at risk.

—Anne Sutton, Executive Principal, St Joseph's Special School, Cranleigh

The rule of law I would almost wholeheartedly support, but of course there are very interesting questions for a Catholic because there are two points at which a Catholic would probably have to say that British law is not something that we would regard as fully just or fully moral. Abortion, which the rule of law upholds, is immoral, so it seems to me for a Catholic that is an injustice supported by the rule of law. So that's problematic. That's one sort of pressure point. The other one I think is same-sex marriage, the whole question of "this is what the law says marriage is" but actually the Catholic Church says something very different. You can run them parallel if you like, but at that point the rule of law says one thing and the Catholic Church says another.

Then of course you've got individual liberty,

which seems to me to be essentially from John Stuart Mill's Ideas on liberty, which is a very important text on liberalism. Mill himself talks about experiments in living and tolerance of minorities, which he wants to protect, so I think for him it is very much, if somebody wants to live a bohemian lifestyle that should be protected from the tyranny of the majority. That idea of protecting minorities but also individual freedom to live as you think fit, whatever that might be, with no kind of necessarily traditional moral understanding. So it is actually quite individualistic potentially and quite libertarian. But far more important for us than individual liberty is the dignity of the human person. That seems to me the foundational idea of John Paul II which all Catholic schools would probably subscribe to as a fundamental principle. It means more than merely the human person being free to do whatever they like. It's founded in the image and likeness of God in everybody and the potential to be a citizen of the kingdom of heaven, if you like. So I think there is, again, a tension potentially there. Or you could say there's a much deeper understanding of human anthropology at work in the dignity of the human person idea, which I would see as much more foundational than individual liberty.

—Hugh Walters, Head of Theology, Downside School, Stratton-on-the-Fosse

I think that you live according to the law of your land and you protest against those rules which you think are wrong. We are very lucky in this society to be able to do that. There are many societies in the world where you can't, so in that sense I think to say British values is respect for the rule of law is absolutely right and within that it would be to protest and to engage. Again, what's absolutely fundamental in terms of Catholic schools is to engage with the community around you and with the wider world and to then realise when things are not as they should be and know how to work for change, that's just Catholic social teaching and everything that we should be about. But that doesn't say don't keep the law, it just says work for change where our law is unjust.

—Charlotte Cummins, Senior Deputy Head, Prior Park College, Bath

We look at other faiths and I would certainly have people in from the local mosque and synagogue and I think that's wonderful, seeing what a religion of love Islam is and having Muslims come in and show how they pray. If we're doing that we are showing tolerance and it's less likely to make any child or young person think that all Muslims are terrorists or Jewish people do this or that because we're actually teaching it properly and saying these are the actual facts, experience it for yourself, let's go to the synagogue, let's go to the mosque, let's talk to the people. And if you're talking about God's love and how we should love one another and be merciful, forgiving people, that's going to happen anyway and it should prevent any extreme behaviour.

—Sarah Conrad, Head of Prep School, St Teresa's, Effingham

Reflections from Early Christian Writing

There are Two Ways: a Way of Life and a Way of Death, and the difference between these two ways is great. The Way of Life is this: Thou shalt love first the Lord thy Creator, and secondly thy neighbour as thyself; and thou shalt do nothing to any man that thou wouldst not wish to be done to thyself. What you may learn from these words is to bless them that curse you, to pray for your enemies, and to fast for your persecutors. For where is the merit in loving only those who return your love? Even the heathens do as much as that. But if you love those who hate you, you will have nobody to be your enemy.

The Way of Death is this… Here are those who persecute good men, hold truth in abhorrence, and love falsehood; who do not know the rewards of righteousness, nor adhere to what is good, nor to just judgement; who lie awake planning wickedness rather than well-doing. Gentleness and patience are beyond their conception, they care for nothing good or useful, and are bent only on their own advantage, without pity for the poor or feeling for the distressed. Knowledge of their Creator is not in them.[37]

from *The Didache* (c. AD 100)

NOTES

NOTES

Chapter 1: Values or Virtues: where do we begin?

1. Sue Palmer, *Toxic Childhood* (London: Orion Books, 2006), 15

2. David Cameron, https://www.gov.uk/government/speeches/pms-speech-on-the-fightback-after-the-riots (accessed 9 April 2016)

3. Cameron, https://www.gov.uk/government/speeches/pms-speech-on-the-fightback-after-the-riots

4. Young Minds Annual Report 2014/15, http://www.youngminds.org.uk/assets/0002/4448/YoungMinds_Annual_Report_14-15.pdf, 4 (accessed 8 April 2016)

5. Young Minds Annual Report 2014/15, http://www.youngminds.org.uk/assets/0002/4448/YoungMinds_Annual_Report_14-15.pdf, 5

6. http://www.youngminds.org.uk/about/whats_the_problem (accessed 8 April 2016)

7. Pope Saint John XXIII, Opening Address to Vatican II, http://www.catholicculture.org/culture/library/view.cfm?RecNum=3233 (accessed 1 June 2016)

8. Pope Saint John XXIII, Opening Address to Vatican II, http://www.catholicculture.org/culture/library/view.cfm?RecNum=3233

9. Pope Francis, *Misericordiae Vultus* ("The Face of Mercy")

10. Pontifical Work for Ecclesiastical Vocations, *New Vocations for a New Europe*, 34

11. Pontifical Work for Ecclesiastical Vocations, *New Vocations for a New Europe*, 11

12. Pontifical Work for Ecclesiastical Vocations, *New Vocations for a New Europe*, 34

13. Pontifical Work for Ecclesiastical Vocations, *New Vocations for a New Europe*, 11

14. Pontifical Work for Ecclesiastical Vocations, *New Vocations for a New Europe*, 11

15. Department for Education, *The Prevent Strategy*, 68

16. Department for Education, *Promoting Fundamental British Values as Part of SMSC in Schools*, 5

17. Department for Education, *Educational Excellence Everywhere*, 94-95

18. *Character Education in UK Schools*, http://www.jubileecentre.ac.uk/userfiles/jubileecentre/pdf/Research%20Reports/Character_Education_in_UK_Schools.pdf, 10 (accessed 7 April 2016)

19. *Character Education in UK Schools*, http://www.jubileecentre.ac.uk/userfiles/jubileecentre/pdf/Research%20Reports/Character_Education_in_UK_Schools.pdf, 4

20. *Character Education in UK Schools*, http://www. jubileecentre.ac.uk/userfiles/jubileecentre/pdf/ Research%20Reports/Character_Education_in_ UK_Schools.pdf, 4

21. *Character Education in UK Schools*, http://www. jubileecentre.ac.uk/userfiles/jubileecentre/pdf/ Research%20Reports/Character_Education_in_ UK_Schools.pdf, 8

22. *Character Education in UK Schools*, http://www. jubileecentre.ac.uk/userfiles/jubileecentre/pdf/ Research%20Reports/Character_Education_in_ UK_Schools.pdf, 9

23. *Catechism of the Catholic Church*, 1803

24. *Catechism of the Catholic Church*, 1804

25. *Catechism of the Catholic Church*, 1811

26. *Catechism of the Catholic Church*, 1811

27. *Catechism of the Catholic Church*, 1812

28. *Catechism of the Catholic Church*, 1827

29. *The Catholic School* (Congregation for Catholic Education), 36

30. Pope Francis, *Evangelii Gaudium* ("The Joy of the Gospel"), 10

31. Marcus Stock, *Christ at the Centre* (London: Catholic Truth Society, 2012), 13

32. Stock, *Christ at the Centre*, 10

33. Stock, *Christ at the Centre*, 15

34. Stock, *Christ at the Centre*, 10, quoting Catechism of the Catholic Church, 1717

35. *The Catholic School*, 55

36. Woolf Institute, *Living with Difference*, 7, http:// www.woolf.cam.ac.uk/uploads/Living%20with%20 Difference.pdf (accessed 7 April 2016)

Chapter 2: Jesus: the parable of God

1. Second Vatican Council, *Dei Verbum* (Dogmatic Constitution on Divine Revelation), 22

2. *Dei Verbum*, Second Vatican Council, 25

3. *Educating Today and Tomorrow: a renewing passion* (Congregation for Catholic Education), III (1a)

4. *Dei Verbum*, Second Vatican Council, 4

5. *Educating Today and Tomorrow*, III

6. *Dei Verbum*, Second Vatican Council, 21

7. Luke Timothy Johnson, *Sacra Pagina: the Gospel of Luke* (Minnesota: Liturgical Press, 1991), 76

8. Johnson, *Sacra Pagina*, 77

9. Johnson, *Sacra Pagina*, 75

10. Johnson, *Sacra Pagina*, 75

11. John P. Meier, *The New Jerome Biblical Commentary* (London: Burns and Oates, 1990), 1320

12. Thomas Keating, *Invitation to Love* (London: Bloomsbury, 2011), 11

13. James Martin SJ, *The Jesuit Guide to (Almost) Everything* (New York: Harper Collins, 2012), 119

14. Martin, *Jesuit Guide to (Almost) Everything*, 120

15. Meier, *New Jerome Biblical Commentary*, 1320

16. Pope Francis, *Misericordiae Vultus* ("The Face of Mercy"), 9

17. James Martin SJ, *Jesus: a pilgrimage* (New York: Harper Collins, 2014), 213

18. Pope Francis, *Misericordiae Vultus*, 6

19. Johnson, *Sacra Pagina*, 242

20. Pheme Perkins, *Reading the New Testament: an introduction* (Mahwah, NJ: Paulist Press, 2012), 221

21. Meier, *New Jerome Biblical Commentary*, 1323

22. Meier, *New Jerome Biblical Commentary*, 1323

23. Martin, *Jesus: a pilgrimage*, 343

24. Raymond E. Brown, *The Origins and the Growth of the Early Johannine Community*, 6-CD set (Ewloe: Welcome Recordings, 2014)

25. *Vatican II: the essential texts* (New York: Image Books, 2012), 214

26. Richard Rohr, *Daily Meditations* (Albuquerque: Centre for Action and Contemplation), 19 May 2016

27. *Catechism of the Catholic Church*, 464

Chapter 3: Gospel Values for Schools: a reading of Luke

1. Marcus Stock, *Christ at the Centre* (London: Catholic Truth Society, 2012), 17

2. Stock, *Christ at the Centre*, 16

3. Pope Francis, *Misericordiae Vultus* ("The Face of Mercy"), 4

4. Luke Timothy Johnson, *Sacra Pagina: the Gospel of Luke* (Minnesota: Liturgical Press, 1991), 175

5. Johnson, *Sacra Pagina*, 175

6. Johnson, *Sacra Pagina*, 112

7. Walter Wink, *Engaging the Powers* (Minneapolis: Fortress Press, 1992), 243

8. James Martin SJ, *Jesus: a pilgrimage* (New York: Harper Collins, 2014), 208

9. Denis McBride C.Ss.R., *The Parables of Jesus* (Chawton: Redemptorist Publications, 1999), 88

10. John P. Meier, *The New Jerome Biblical Commentary* (London: Burns and Oates, 1990), 1243

11. Pope Francis, *Evangelii Gaudium* ("The Joy of the Gospel"), 2

12. Johnson, *Sacra Pagina*, 106

13. Jean Vanier, *Signs of the Times* (London: Darton, Longman and Todd, 2013), 6

14. Vanier, *Signs of the Times*, 27

15. Vanier, *Signs of the Times*, 55

16. Geza Vermes, *Christian Beginnings: from Nazareth to Nicaea, AD 30–325* (London: Penguin Books, 2012), 56

17. Vermes, *Christian Beginnings*, 56

18. Johnson, *Sacra Pagina*, 274

19. Johnson, *Sacra Pagina*, 274

20. Johnson, *Sacra Pagina*, 274

21. Johnson, *Sacra Pagina*, 108

22. Martin, *Jesus: a pilgrimage*, 258

23. Martin, *Jesus: a pilgrimage*, 258

24. Raymond E. Brown SS, *101 Questions on the Bible* (New York: Paulist Press, 1990), 66

25. Johnson, *Sacra Pagina*, 258

26. Johnson, *Sacra Pagina*, 111

27. Johnson, *Sacra Pagina*, 389

Chapter 4: Eight Signs of a Gospel-inspired School

1. Second Vatican Council, *Gaudium et Spes* (Pastoral Constitution on the Church in the Modern World), 3

2. Second Vatican Council, *Gaudium et Spes*, 29

3. Archbishop J. Michael Miller CSB, *The Holy See's Teaching on Catholic Schools* (Manchester, NH: Sophia Institute Press, 2006), 21

4. Dermot Lane, *Catholic Education in the Light of Vatican II and Laudato Si'* (Dublin: Veritas Publications, 2015), 28

5. *The Catholic School* (Congregation for Catholic Education, 1977), 46

6. *The Catholic School*, 34

7. Sean Whittle, *A Theory of Catholic Education* (London: Bloomsbury, 2015), 86

8. *Educating Today and Tomorrow: a renewing passion* (Congregation for Catholic Education), III (1g)

9. *Educating Today and Tomorrow*, III (1g)

10. *Educating Today and Tomorrow*, III

11. Miller, *The Holy See's Teaching on Catholic Schools*, 26

12. Second Vatican Council, *Gravissimum Educationis* ("The Declaration on Christian Education"), 8

13. Miller, *The Holy See's Teaching on Catholic Schools*, vii

14. Miller, *The Holy See's Teaching on Catholic Schools*, 30

15. Saint Pope John Paul II, *Novo Millennio Inuente* ("At the Beginning of the New Millennium"), 43

16. Saint Pope John Paul II, *Novo Millennio Inuente*, 43

17. "Consecrated Persons and Their Mission in Schools" (Congregation for Catholic Education, 2002), 46

18. "Consecrated Persons and Their Mission in Schools", 46

19. *The Catholic School*, 37

20. Whittle, *A Theory of Catholic Education*, 86

21. "The Religious Dimension of Education" (Congregation for Catholic Education, 1988), 69

22. "The Religious Dimension of Education", 69

23. For the most recent figures on the slow decline of the Catholicity of staff in Catholic schools, see the Catholic Education Service's Digest of 2015 Census Data for Schools and Colleges in England.

24. Second Vatican Council, *Gravissimum Educationis*, 1

25. Second Vatican Council, *Gravissimum Educationis*, 1

26. Final Statement of the World Congress for Educating Today and Tomorrow: A Renewing Passion, http://www.educatio.va/content/cec/it/congregazione-per-l-educazione-cattolica/attivita/comunicato-finale-del-congresso-mondiale--educare-oggi-e-domani-.html (accessed 23 December 2015)

27. *Educating Today and Tomorrow*, III (1e)

28. Second Vatican Council, *Gravissimum Educationis*, 9

29. Second Vatican Council, *Gravissimum Educationis*, 8

30. Second Vatican Council, *Gravissimum Educationis*, 9

31. Whittle, *A Theory of Catholic Education*, 38

32. *The Catholic School on the Threshold of the Third Millennium* (Congregation for Catholic Education, 1997), 15

33. *The Catholic School on the Threshold of the Third Millennium*, 15

34. *The Catholic School on the Threshold of the Third Millennium*, 15

35. *The Catholic School on the Threshold of the Third Millennium*, 15

36. *Educating Today and Tomorrow*, II (5)

37. Second Vatican Council, *Gravissimum Educationis*, 3

38. *The Catholic School*, 58

39. *The Catholic School*, 56

40. *Educating Today and Tomorrow*, III (1e)

41. Thomas H. Groome, *Christian Religious Education: sharing our story and vision* (San Francisco: Jossey-Bass, 1980), 264

42. Marcus Stock, *Christ at the Centre* (London: Catholic Truth Society, 2012), 13

43. Pontifical Work for Ecclesiastical Vocations, *New Vocations for a New Europe*, 13a

44. Pontifical Work for Ecclesiastical Vocations, *New Vocations for a New Europe*, 17a

45. Pontifical Work for Ecclesiastical Vocations, *New Vocations for a New Europe*, 13a

46. Pope Benedict XVI, *Celebration of Catholic Education*, 2010, https://w2.vatican.va/content/benedict-xvi/en/speeches/2010/september/documents/hf_ben-xvi_spe_20100917_mondo-educ.html (accessed 1 May 2016)

47. Second Vatican Council, *Gaudium et Spes*, 41

48. Pope Paul VI, "Address to Members of the Consilium de Laicis", 2 October 1974

Chapter 5: Eight Signs of Gospel-inspired Leadership

1. *Educating Today and Tomorrow: a renewing passion* (Congregation for Catholic Education), III (1b)

2. *Educating Today and Tomorrow*, III (1b)

3. Marcus Stock, *Christ at the Centre* (London: Catholic Truth Society, 2012), 27

4. Stock, *Christ at the Centre*, 34

5. Richard Rohr, *Falling Upward: a spirituality for the two halves of life* (San Francisco: Jossey-Bass, 2011), x

6. Thomas Keating, *Open Mind, Open Heart: the contemplative dimension of the Gospel* (London: Bloomsbury, 2006), 24

7. Keating, *Open Mind, Open Heart*, 48

8. Pope Paul VI, *Evangelii Nuntiandi* ("Evangelisation in our Time"), 10

9. Second Vatican Council, *Unitatis Redintegratio* ("Decree on Ecumenism"), 1

10. Stock, *Christ at the Centre*, 19

11. Richard Wilkin, "Interpreting the Tradition", Networking, 15(4), April 2014

12. Pope John XXIII, Opening Address to Vatican Council II

13. Thomas Keating, *Invitation to Love* (London, Bloomsbury, 2011), 148

14. Second Vatican Council, *Gravissimum Educationis*, ("Declaration on Christian Education"), 1

15. Second Vatican Council, *Gaudium et Spes*, ("Pastoral Constitution on the Church in the Modern World"), 4

16. Office for National Statistics, *Divorce in England and Wales 2013*, http://www.ons.gov.uk/peoplepopulationandcommunity/birthsdeathsandmarriages/divorce/bulletins/divorcesinenglandandwales/2013 (accessed 3 August 2016)

17. It is also worth saying that part of the role of the outward-facing head teacher is to protect the school from philosophies and ideologies which would be contrary to the school's values.

18. Carol Dweck, "Mindset: what is Mindset", http://mindsetonline.com/whatisit/about/index.html (accessed 3 August 2016)

19. John Sullivan, *Catholic Schools in Contention: competing metaphors and leadership implications* (Dublin: Lindisfarne Books, 2000), 109

20. *The Catholic School*, 58

21. Sullivan, *Catholic Schools in Contention*, 109

22. Sullivan, *Catholic Schools in Contention*, 155

23. Sullivan, *Catholic Schools in Contention*, 155

24. Sean Ruth, *Leadership and Liberation: a psychological approach* (Hove: Routledge, 2006), 53

25. Catholic leaders should also be wary of the opposite of best thinking, which might be termed "bad thinking". This is when you give in to those compulsive negative scripts, usually involving sensitive reactions to imagined slights or imagined dialogues with colleagues that you are determined to win! Remember: most conflict takes place in your head. Such thinking can be a real drain on your energy.

26. Ruth, *Leadership and Liberation*, 6

27. Pope Francis, Presentation of the Christmas Greetings to the Roman Curia, http://w2.vatican.va/content/francesco/en/speeches/2014/december/documents/papa-francesco_20141222_curia-romana.html (accessed 10 January 2015)

28. Ruth, *Leadership and Liberation*, 9

29. Code of Canon Law, 806

30. The Catholic Bishops of England and Wales, "Catholic Education in England and Wales", 3

Chapter 6: Forming Good Citizens: notes towards a civilisation of love

1. Catholic Education Service, *Catholic Values and "British Values": practical advice from the Catholic Education Service*, February 2015

2. *The Catholic School* (Congregation for Catholic Education), 37

3. Ofsted, *School Inspection Handbook* (August 2015), 42

4. *Catechism of the Catholic Church*, 1965

5. *Catechism of the Catholic Church*, 1965

6. *Catechism of the Catholic Church*, 1968

7. *Catechism of the Catholic Church*, 1972

8. *Catechism of the Catholic Church*, 1972

9. *Catechism of the Catholic Church*, 1974

10. *Catechism of the Catholic Church*, 1967

11. Department for Education, *The Prevent Duty: departmental advice for schools and childcare providers* (2015), 3

12. Department for Education, *The Prevent Duty*, 6

13. Cardinal Vincent Nichols, Address to CATSC Conference, January 2016

14. Cardinal Vincent Nichols, Address to CATSC Conference

15. Cardinal Vincent Nichols, Address to CATSC Conference

16. Cardinal Vincent Nichols, Address to CATSC Conference

17. Pope Leo XIII, *Spectata Fides* ("Outstanding Faith"), 4

18. Pope Leo XIII, *Spectata Fides*, 5

19. Pope Leo XIII, *Spectata Fides*, 6

20. Pope Pius XI, *Divini Illius Magistri* ("On the Christian Education of Youth"), 60

21. Pope Pius XI, *Divini Illius Magistri*, 59

22. Pope Pius XI, *Divini Illius Magistri*, 53

23. Pope Pius XI, *Divini Illius Magistri*, 97

24. *School Inspection Handbook*, 36

25. Catholic Education Service, *Catholic Values and "British Values": the background to the debate on "British values"* (updated September 2015)

26. Catholic Education Service, *Catholic Values and "British Values"*

27. *Living with Difference* (Cambridge: Woolf Institute, 2015), 8

28. *Educating to Intercultural Dialogue in Catholic Schools: living in harmony for a civilization of love* (Congregation for Catholic Education 2013), 11

29. *Educating to Intercultural Dialogue*, 11

30. *Educating to Intercultural Dialogue*, 11

31. Rupert Shortt, *God is No Thing* (London: Hurst & Company, 2016), 3

32. *Educating to Intercultural Dialogue*, 20

33. *Educating to Intercultural Dialogue*, 66

34. *Educating to Intercultural Dialogue*, 41

35. "French Bishops Declare Day of Fasting After Priest's Murder", http://www.catholicnewsagency.com/news/french-bishops-declare-day-of-fasting-after-priests-murder-24511/ (accessed 2 August 2016)

36. "French Bishops Declare Day of Fasting After Priest's Murder"

37. Maxwell Staniforth (trans.), *Early Christian Writings* (London: Penguin Books, 1968), 191, 193